HOW OBAMA & THE DEMOCRATS MAY HAVE STOLEN THE 2012 ELECTION

by Mark Steffen

DORRANCE
PUBLISHING CO
EST. 1920
PITTSBURGH, PENNSYLVANIA 15238

Dorrance Publishing Co
585 Alpha Drive
Pittsburgh, PA 15238
Visit our website at *www.dorrancebookstore.com*

ISBN: 978-1-6366-1537-0
eISBN: 978-1-6366-1550-9

HOW OBAMA & THE DEMOCRATS MAY HAVE STOLEN THE 2012 ELECTION

Foreword

From The Author:

This book was written in the year following the 2012 election. For me, many things about the outcome didn't seem to add up, so I decided to look into it and see if my feelings were valid. I spent the next 12 months researching actual election results, reports of voting irregularities, fund raising, computer issues, and use of the federal government to influence the outcome.

Today, millions of Americans are voicing concerns and questions about the legitimacy of the presidential election in November and the Senate elections in January in Georgia. I think you'll see in this book that many of the problems and issues seen in these recent elections were also very much a part of the election in 2012. You'll also see that 2012 was not the first time these things happened by any means.

My greatest hope is that this book serves to illustrate a very important point - that voter fraud really does exist, and that it isn't random or rare as many would have you believe. Most importantly, I think you will realize that the problem is getting worse, not better, with each subsequent election, and that we are on a path to where America may never see another honest and fair election unless something is done.

Make no mistake, there are many in this country who seek that very outcome, who want to ensure the outcome of our elections before any vote is even cast, regardless of whether or not that outcome reflects the legitimate will of the American people. Based on what I've seen, I believe that's what happened in both 2012 and 2020. After reading this book, we'll see what you think.

As we're all now painfully aware, Barack Obama was declared to have won reelection on November 6, 2012. I didn't say "Barack Obama won reelection on November 6" because I'm not entirely sure that's what really happened.

For the record, it was reported that Obama collected just over 51% of the vote, with 62,611,250 votes, while Mitt Romney received 59,134,475*. The final electoral count was Obama 332, Romney 206. This is being touted by many on the left as a convincing victory, a mandate for Obama, possibly even a landslide.

In truth, it was anything but. If Mitt Romney had received just 333,908 more votes in the states of Ohio, Virginia, Florida, and New Hampshire, he would now be the President, with an electoral victory of 270–268. Romney could easily have won Pennsylvania, and in fact did minus just one county, which would have made the electoral total 290–258 in his favor.

This was, in reality, an extraordinarily close election, and in fact only a very small number of voters in just a few states gave Obama his electoral victory. The facts are:

- Obama won Ohio by only 166,000 votes, with one county—Cuyahoga County—providing him a 236,000-vote margin. In 144 precincts in that county, there were roughly 75,000 votes for Obama and less than 500 votes for Romney. The same kind of margins were seen in precincts in Hamilton County, where dozens of unregistered voters were allowed to illegally cast ballots, and charges of voter fraud were filed against a number of voters, including a nun who voted for a dead colleague.

*in terms of the final national election results, you will find any number of "final" vote tally's reported by various news agencies.

- Obama only won Florida by 72,989 votes. As you will see, a very tiny portion of only two counties provided him with his winning margin, by providing him with overwhelming percentages of the vote, and in precincts where all manner of irregularities were observed by Republican poll watchers, not to mention the fact that votes were possibly switched.
- In Pennsylvania, Obama won by about 309,000 votes, but he had a margin of 467,000 votes in one county—Philadelphia County—where several Divisions saw their Republican poll watchers removed for several hours and then registered over 99% of the vote for Obama, including 59 divisions with zero Romney votes.
- Obama won Virginia by 115,910 votes. Only 78 precincts out of 2,584 in the state, 3% of the precincts and all from city jurisdictions, provided Obama over 70% of his winning margin. We were treated there to a video of a Democratic Congressman's son giving lessons on how to commit voter fraud, and again had reports from poll watchers of massive voter fraud.

What's listed above is really just scratching the surface. What happened in some of these states, and more specifically in certain precincts, is truly amazing. You've heard the saying "the devil is in the details"? That certainly applies here.

So how did they do it? How did Obama win despite:

- Unemployment of over 7%, the first President EVER to win reelection above that threshold.
- An abysmal economy, and a nearly trillion dollar "stimulus" bill that did nothing to improve the economy as he'd promised.
- A skyrocketing debt that topped $16 trillion, over $6 trillion of that added in Obama's first term.
- The scandals in Fast & Furious where, for the first time ever, an Attorney General was held in Contempt of Congress.
- Gas prices that were double what they were when Obama took office.
- Food prices that had risen every month since June of 2010.
- Obama's assault on freedom of religion.

- Obama's lack of respect for our Constitution and the separation of powers.
- Obama's open hostility toward Israel.
- The very unpopular ObamaCare.
- Obama's unpopular and unconstitutional implementation of the Dream Act (which Congress rejected).
- Eric Holder's appointment of known Obama supporters to investigate White House National Security leaks.
- The disgraceful handling of the Benghazi attacks, where our ambassador and three other Americans were murdered while Obama apparently played cards.

Conventional wisdom tells us that historically any *one* of the above could be enough to derail a Presidential reelection bid. With all of them combined, especially the "pocketbook" issues—high unemployment, high gas prices, high food prices—many experts would have told you that Obama should have gone the way of the former worst president ever, Jimmy Carter. Yet, somehow, Obama got reelected. The real question is "how?", and the much larger question is:

Was Barack Obama *legitimately* reelected in November of 2012?

In short, I believe the answer is no. I believe there's substantial evidence to support my thesis that the Obama reelection team and Democratic Party employed both tried and true as well as some new and innovative (and frightening) strategies to allow them to hold on to the presidency.

At the end of the day, what it ultimately came down to was a combination of massive voter fraud along with abusing the power of the White House in order to hold on to that power.

The Democratic Party and voter fraud have starred together in elections across the country for decades, but nowhere more often than the city Obama calls home—Chicago. Many would consider Chicago to be the very birthplace of voter fraud, and the Democratic Voter Fraud Playbook, employed many times by Democrats in Chicago and elsewhere, has always had five basic tenants:

1. Get as many "registered voters" as possible on the voter rolls, legitimate or otherwise.
2. Ensure that all of those "registered voters," legitimate or otherwise, living or dead, are never removed from the voter rolls.
3. Ensure that someone shows up on Election Day (or before, or both) and votes under the names of all of those "registered voters," legitimate or otherwise.
4. Fight against requirement of a photo ID, or any other potential roadblocks to voter fraud, to include the removal or blocked admission of Republican poll watchers whenever possible.
5. Label anyone who makes any attempt to reduce voter fraud as nothing more than a racist.

The above tactics have proven effective for Democrats in an untold number of elections, but Obama and his team wanted to hedge their bets. They decided to add, or at least certainly enhance, five more very powerful and very chilling strategies to help ensure Obama's reelection in 2012:

6. Buy votes, by promising to give as much money as possible to as many people as possible for as many things as possible.
7. Bring in donations from anywhere and everywhere, legal or otherwise.
8. Utilize the full force and intimidation of the United States government, primarily the IRS, to harass and suppress the efforts of their political opponents.
9. Use the new technology available, such as electronic voting machines, to their advantage whenever possible.
10. Ensure that everyone who was willing to conduct any of the above activities on their behalf knew that they could do so with impunity, that they could carry out these activities without fear of prosecution.

We'll call this list the "Chicago Ten," in honor of the rich heritage Chicago has in voting irregularities, and in honor of their current favorite son who has taken these practices to a whole new level.

Throughout the course of this book, I'll show you examples of how the Obama team and Democrats carried out the above strategies, providing specific examples of each to support my theory—that Barack Obama did not legitimately, or legally, win the White House.

In the interest of full disclosure, I was very much against the reelection of Barack Obama, and given that you bought this book I assume you felt the same. It's also therefore likely that in the days following November 6, 2012, you experienced the same shock, disillusionment, and outright fear for our country that I did.

I was very surprised on election night when Ohio went for Obama. Living just across the Ohio River from Cincinnati, I'd heard radio accounts all day long about massive turnout in Republican precincts throughout Cincinnati and in other parts of Southern Ohio. When I arrived to vote at my own (very conservative) northern Kentucky precinct at 6:00 a.m., there were nearly 80 people already in line. This was in stark contrast to the eight people in line at the same time in 2008. (My precinct incidentally went 752–225 for Romney).

For three months prior to the election, I knocked on doors in Hamilton County (Cincinnati), and saw firsthand the enthusiasm of people who couldn't wait to vote for Mitt Romney. Everything I saw, everything I read in the polls, and most importantly everything I heard on Election Day pointed toward a Romney win in Ohio, and thus for the presidency. When that didn't happen, I was distraught, mainly out of fear for what this country will look like ten or twenty years from now for my children and grandchildren.

When I saw just how close the vote turned out to be in Ohio, I started looking into it. What bothered me most, and the reason I ultimately decided to write this book after examining some of the numbers, is that it seemed clear to me that the will of the people of Ohio was not served on November 6. Looking at a few other states, I believe the same can be said there as well.

In case you're wondering who I am or what my qualifications are to write this book, my only real title in that regard is "concerned father and citizen." I'm not a politician (though I was a City Councilman in my small town for a few years; trust me that doesn't count). I'm not an author or a reporter, and I'm not an active member of any state or county political party. I'm just an ordinary citizen.

In addition to laying out how I believe Obama won this election, I thought this book could serve as a reference for others who may not have the time to keep up with things as much as they'd like. I also wanted to illustrate that all of this information is readily accessible for anyone, even ordinary citizens, who want to learn more.

I did all the research for this book myself, sitting at my home computer and finding on-line virtually everything you'll read on these pages. Thanks to the power of the internet, we are no longer at the mercy of the network news organizations, and anyone at least as computer literate as I am (which is pretty much everyone) can be as informed as they want to be.

I've also tried to add some historical perspective on what's happened in elections in the past, and have included many examples of Democratic Party chicanery that perhaps you'd not heard of before. Again, thanks to the wonder of the internet, there is nothing contained in this book that you can't look up for yourself.

In the days and months after the election I worried and prayed every day about the direction Obama would take this country. I knew in my heart that if we continued down the path Obama had planned for America, if we followed his vision for the future, the great country I was blessed to grow up in won't be there for future generations. I finally decided to stop just complaining about it, to stop watching America slip away, and to do something about it. That something, for whatever it's worth, was writing this book.

What will follow is a review of how the Obama reelection team executed the above ten strategies. You'll see examples of their efforts to illegitimately register voters, how they fought against cleaning up voter rolls, and how they fought desperately in many states against voter ID laws. You'll see many examples of literally unbelievable voter totals for Obama in key battleground states, and some of the things they did to get those numbers. You will see examples of how this administration utilized the power of the federal government to harass, threaten, and thwart its political opponents, and the depths they sank to in order to raise money. You will read about the distinct possibility that votes were actually switched, the worst kind of voter fraud of all. And finally, you will see how Eric Holder used his office to help protect their voter fraud franchise, and made sure that everyone involved knew that no one would be held accountable.

Everything you will read here, in terms of the election results in specific states, counties, divisions, wards, and precincts, came directly from the county and state websites which are reported on. I'm sure there'll be those who will attack my conclusions, and my opinions, but everything you read, in terms of the election results outlined herein, can easily be found online by anyone who wants to do so.

I'm going to start with a review of some of the key battleground states that ultimately made the difference for Obama. As I review these key states, I will touch on specific examples of how I think Democrats and the Obama administration orchestrated their ten strategies to steal the 2012 election.

OHIO

I'm starting with Ohio because anyone who remotely followed the election knew that Ohio was the one state that both Mitt Romney and Barack Obama had to win. This turned out to be true, when late in the evening on election night the networks declared Barack Obama the winner in Ohio, and as such that he'd been reelected.

When the final results were in, Barack Obama won Ohio by a narrow margin, with 2,827,621 votes versus 2,661,407 for Romney. The map below shows the Obama counties in light shade, the Romney counties in dark.

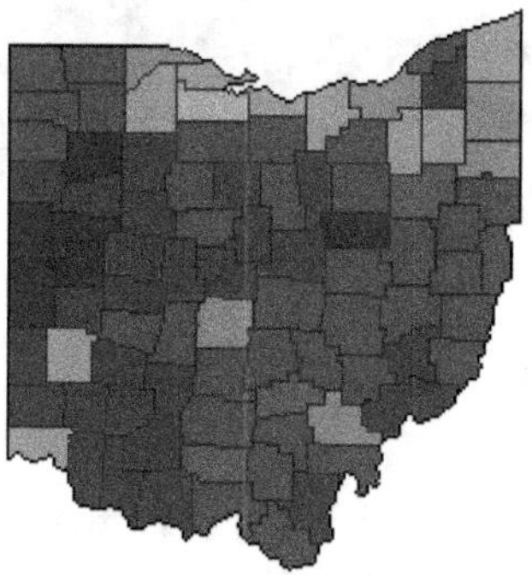

Collecting 51.5% of the vote in Ohio, Obama's margin of victory was only 166,214 votes out of about 5.5 million votes cast. Even though the above map shows 71 out of 88 counties going for Mitt Romney*, Obama won the state with heavy margins in just a handful of counties. The counties carried by

Obama either contained a large metropolitan area, a university, as in the case of Athens County (lower right), or both. This will become a common theme, and you'll see other pictures of other states that look very much like the one above, as we review the handful of states that led to the reelection of Barack Obama.

The eight counties in Ohio that showed heavy margins for Obama and that gave him the state, were:

- Cuyahoga County, where Obama tallied 447,232 votes to 190,651 for Romney, a margin of 256,581 votes. This alone was well more than Obama's total state margin of 166,214 (actually 154% of it).
- Franklin County, which provided 346,336 votes for Obama to 215,987 for Romney, another 130,349-vote margin, equaling almost 80% of his margin statewide.
- Lucas County, which registered 136,161 votes for Obama, only 69,940 for Romney, a margin of 66,676.
- Summit County (+42,037), Mahoning County (+34,418), Trumbull County (+23,393) and Lorain County (+22,059) combined for an additional margin of 121,907.
- Hamilton County in southern Ohio, long a Republican stronghold, also went slightly for Obama.

These eight counties registered 602,114 more votes for Barack Obama than they gave to Mitt Romney. Which means:

Barack Obama lost the other 80 counties of Ohio by a total of 435,900 votes, or by about 8%.

Bad as that may seem, it's even worse than that:

If you take out just one, Cuyahoga County, the other 87 Ohio counties, including the other 16 that voted for Obama, elected

Mitt Romney by about 90,000 votes, or 1.6% of the vote.

You read that right. Take out 1 of 88 counties, Romney wins Ohio by 1.6%.

The above eight counties account for roughly 2.45 million votes, or about 45% of the total statewide vote. What you are about to see is why the remaining 55% of the voters—which went heavily for Romney—weren't able to offset Obama's margins in these eight counties. Obama prevailed because a tiny fraction of Ohio voters—*just a small number of precincts*—gave Obama not only very high numbers, but gave them to him in absolutely incredible percentages.

Incredible, as in not credible, is the operative word, and you'll find this to be a recurring theme throughout this book. To show you just how incredible, we're going to focus on four of the above counties—Cuyahoga, Franklin, Lucas, and Hamilton—and show you how just a small fraction of the voters in these four counties were enough to win the state for Barack Obama.

Cuyahoga County is located in the far northeastern part of the state and encompasses the city of Cleveland. I've already shown you that this county alone was enough to give the state to Obama, but how that happened is the real story. Everyone knew Cuyahoga County would be strong for Obama, but I'm not sure anyone expected, or whether we can believe, the vote totals that were recorded for Obama in many of these precincts.

You may have seen reports that there were 9 precincts in Cuyahoga County that gave Mitt Romney zero votes. I actually found 17, but that's just the tip of the iceberg. Believe it or not:

More than 100 precincts in Cuyahoga County gave Barack Obama more than 99% of the vote.

There were 133, to be precise, that gave Obama 99%+ of the vote. Following are the results from those and 11 others, 144 precincts in all. These come direct from the Cuyahoga County Board of Elections, showing the respective number of votes for Barack Obama and Mitt Romney, the resulting margin and the percentage captured for Obama, starting with those where Romney received zero votes:

Precinct	Obama	Romney	Margin	% for Obama
154	579	0	579	100.0%
192	423	0	423	100.0%
204	637	0	637	100.0%
205	534	0	534	100.0%
206	286	0	286	100.0%
219	416	0	416	100.0%
228	425	0	425	100.0%
232	72	0	72	100.0%
233	436	0	436	100.0%
241	123	0	123	100.0%
242	123	0	123	100.0%
248	374	0	374	100.0%
273	501	0	501	100.0%
280	52	0	52	100.0%
285	452	0	452	100.0%
288	493	0	493	100.0%
523	515	0	515	100.0%
185	571	1	570	99.8%
144	567	1	566	99.8%
276	537	1	536	99.8%
289	514	1	513	99.8%
315	499	1	498	99.8%
118	486	1	485	99.8%
512	482	1	481	99.8%
190	455	1	454	99.8%
290	434	1	433	99.8%
287	423	1	422	99.8%
274	421	1	420	99.8%
279	413	1	412	99.8%
200	406	1	405	99.8%
312	397	1	396	99.7%
314	352	1	351	99.7%
284	351	1	350	99.7%
222	677	2	675	99.7%
148	673	2	671	99.7%
136	667	2	665	99.7%
153	596	2	594	99.7%
526	596	2	594	99.7%
183	595	2	593	99.7%
147	582	2	580	99.7%
149	565	2	563	99.6%
120	564	2	562	99.6%
225	556	2	554	99.6%
194	549	2	547	99.6%
155	544	2	542	99.6%
188	540	2	538	99.6%
187	533	2	531	99.6%
272	510	2	508	99.6%

211	506	2	504	99.6%
269	504	2	502	99.6%
311	500	2	498	99.6%
516	489	2	487	99.6%
256	473	2	471	99.6%
249	469	2	467	99.6%
253	465	2	463	99.6%
278	460	2	458	99.6%
152	653	3	650	99.5%
151	649	3	646	99.5%
195	636	3	633	99.5%
186	618	3	615	99.5%
615	412	2	410	99.5%
145	614	3	611	99.5%
184	614	3	611	99.5%
130	809	4	805	99.5%
262	394	2	392	99.5%
133	775	4	771	99.5%
513	383	2	381	99.5%
217	382	2	380	99.5%
221	756	4	752	99.5%
124	565	3	562	99.5%
157	562	3	559	99.5%
250	374	2	372	99.5%
226	366	2	364	99.5%
127	724	4	720	99.5%
270	543	3	540	99.5%
275	540	3	537	99.4%
189	535	3	532	99.4%
126	712	4	708	99.4%
213	350	2	348	99.4%
234	338	2	336	99.4%
520	500	3	497	99.4%
240	166	1	165	99.4%
302	494	3	491	99.4%
121	488	3	485	99.4%
132	648	4	644	99.4%
317	475	3	472	99.4%
134	786	5	781	99.4%
519	314	2	312	99.4%
196	465	3	462	99.4%
203	618	4	614	99.4%
210	453	3	450	99.3%
227	435	3	432	99.3%
271	578	4	574	99.3%
122	719	5	714	99.3%
320	696	5	691	99.3%
282	555	4	551	99.3%
191	549	4	545	99.3%

150	547	4	543	99.3%
193	532	4	528	99.3%
518	395	3	392	99.2%
303	505	4	501	99.2%
128	495	4	491	99.2%
156	495	4	491	99.2%
223	494	4	490	99.2%
511	370	3	367	99.2%
199	738	6	732	99.2%
135	733	6	727	99.2%
123	731	6	725	99.2%
521	487	4	483	99.2%
254	485	4	481	99.2%
294	485	4	481	99.2%
216	484	4	480	99.2%
261	482	4	478	99.2%
142	475	4	471	99.2%
119	593	5	588	99.2%
236	472	4	468	99.2%
251	472	4	468	99.2%
510	448	4	444	99.1%
307	447	4	443	99.1%
218	552	5	547	99.1%
514	329	3	326	99.1%
292	436	4	432	99.1%
515	427	4	423	99.1%
259	531	5	526	99.1%
310	519	5	514	99.0%
258	518	5	513	99.0%
229	511	5	506	99.0%
131	814	8	806	99.0%
522	605	6	599	99.0%
230	496	5	491	99.0%
286	586	6	580	99.0%
125	776	8	768	99.0%
207	384	4	380	99.0%
212	375	4	371	98.9%
24	616	7	609	98.9%
531	1032	12	1020	98.9%
509	567	7	560	98.8%
137	711	9	702	98.8%
592	663	9	654	98.7%
146	622	9	613	98.6%
146	622	9	613	98.6%
129	748	11	737	98.6%
593	579	9	570	98.5%
143	567	10	557	98.3%
TOTALS	**74556**	**452**	**74104**	**99.4%**

I apologize for the long list, but the mind-boggling results we can take from it are:

- The above 144 precincts cast a total of **74,556** votes for Barack Obama, ***and only 452*** for Mitt Romney.
- That is an *average vote of **518 – 3*** per precinct, with Obama receiving **99.4%** of the vote.
- Romney reached double figures in only three of the above 144 precincts, garnering 10, 11, and 12 votes.
- This margin of 74,014 votes (out of 75,008 cast) *in just these 144 precincts represents about 45% of Obama's statewide winning margin of 166,214.*
- In the rest of Cuyahoga County, Obama received 66% of the vote, yet in these precincts, he received about 99%—*a full 50% higher*.

The voters in these 144 precincts represent only about 11% of the voters in the county, and only comprise about 1.4% of the total voting population of Ohio. And yet, we're asked to believe that somehow this 1.4% of the voters was able to generate 45% of Obama's winning margin in Ohio. I want to be sure that sinks in:

> 1.4% of the state's voters is said to have given Barack Obama
> about 45% of his winning margin in the state.
> Does that seem out of proportion to anyone besides me?

Again, 133 of the 144 above 33 precincts recorded over 99% of the vote for Barack Obama, and the other eleven were over 98%. While that certainly isn't completely impossible, it's close. Below is a map of all of Cuyahoga County from the Board of Elections that was published in The Plain Dealer. As you can see, there are parts of the county where Romney did well, and where he received a percentage of the vote more in line with state and national norms.

Cuyahoga County vote

The precinct-by-precinct presidential vote in Cuyahoga County illustrates the core of the Democratic Party's strength.

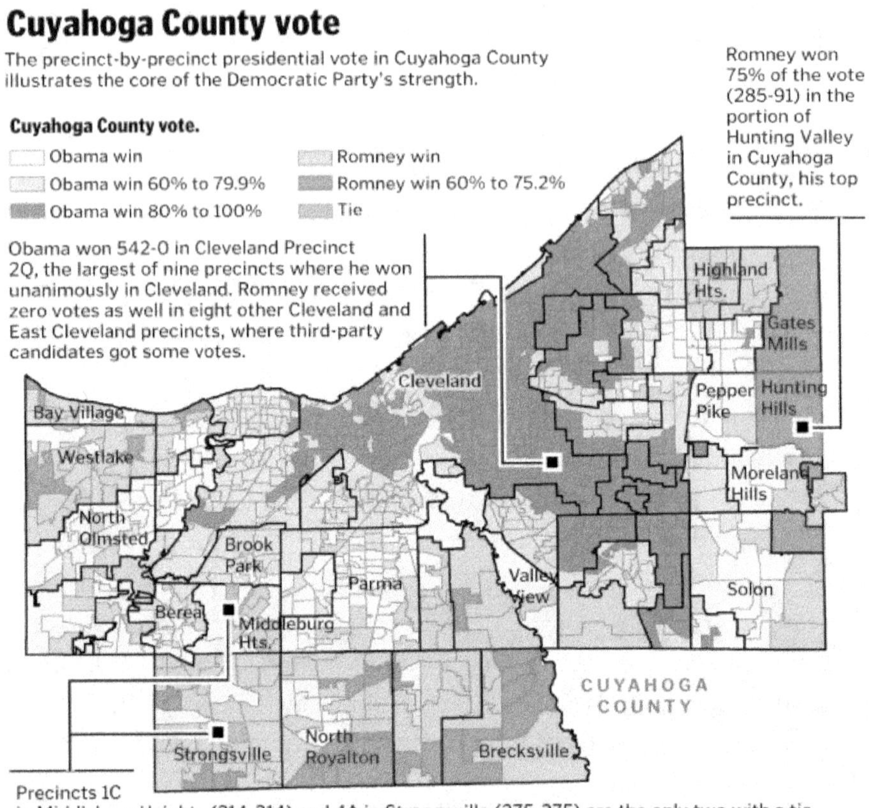

in Middleburg Heights (214-214) and 4A in Strongsville (275-275) are the only two with a tie.

SOURCE: Cuyahoga County Board of Elections

RICH EXNER, JAMES OWENS | THE PLAIN DEALER

There's a lot of blue on that map, but there's a lot of red as well. I realize it's not unusual to see different results in different parts of a county, but 50% different?

Next stop is Franklin County, situated in the central part of Ohio and containing the state capital of Columbus. Franklin County at one time had been more of a Republican county, but in recent years it's trended more Democratic. Much of this trend has been driven by the university and the vote in the central part of the city.

There are 801 precincts in Franklin County, and 562,323 votes were cast either for Barack Obama or Mitt Romney. Of those votes, Barack Obama won 62% and 346,336 votes, with Romney winning 38% and 215,987 votes. This was good for a winning margin for Obama of 130,349 votes.

Just as we saw in Cuyahoga County, this margin was largely driven by a very small number of precincts and voters. The 72 precincts in Franklin

County that drove the winning margin for Barack Obama, and the results for those precincts, are as follows:

	Obama	Romney
COLUMBUS 02-A	483	52
COLUMBUS 56-D	1,312	34
COLUMBUS 83-D	1,180	99
COLUMBUS 83-C	1,040	57
COLUMBUS 83-F	981	24
COLUMBUS 83-E	942	62
COLUMBUS 44-E	903	70
COLUMBUS 05-B	931	21
COLUMBUS 17-B	877	14
COLUMBUS 25-C	858	14
COLUMBUS 07-C	827	14
COLUMBUS 26-B	780	41
COLUMBUS 44-A	751	42
COLUMBUS 51-A	734	39
COLUMBUS 48-E	714	56
COLUMBUS 48-C	708	59
COLUMBUS 35-B	748	16
COLUMBUS 48-A	668	82
COLUMBUS 55-C	707	39
COLUMBUS 51-C	699	46
COLUMBUS 06-B	709	31
COLUMBUS 25-E	720	12
COLUMBUS 44-D	662	56
COLUMBUS 35-C	696	16
COLUMBUS 25-B	676	33
COLUMBUS 28-A	671	34
COLUMBUS 25-D	674	15
COLUMBUS 06-C	669	16
COLUMBUS 56-C	641	43
COLUMBUS 48-D	626	57
COLUMBUS 56-A	630	44
COLUMBUS 25-H	609	50
COLUMBUS 26-A	628	27
COLUMBUS 25-F	626	27
COLUMBUS 44-C	621	31
COLUMBUS 47-B	598	39
COLUMBUS 52-D	565	63
COLUMBUS 55-B	575	51
COLUMBUS 44-B	574	45
COLUMBUS 28-B	580	35
COLUMBUS 52-E	574	40
COLUMBUS 35-D	591	20
COLUMBUS 50-A	590	15
COLUMBUS 35-A	569	32

COLUMBUS 55-D	528	72
COLUMBUS 13-D	580	15
COLUMBUS 04-D	563	23
COLUMBUS 06-D	546	39
COLUMBUS 06-A	551	19
COLUMBUS 07-D	540	26
COLUMBUS 51-B	498	65
COLUMBUS 51-D	532	29
COLUMBUS 04-B	509	34
COLUMBUS 56-B	501	36
COLUMBUS 13-B	511	14
COLUMBUS 68-B	478	46
COLUMBUS 03-A	503	14
COLUMBUS 07-B	484	23
COLUMBUS 17-D	497	6
COLUMBUS 04-A	474	28
COLUMBUS 05-A	474	27
COLUMBUS 13-C	492	6
COLUMBUS 06-E	486	11
COLUMBUS 06-F	458	16
COLUMBUS 04-C	456	17
COLUMBUS 48-B	422	41
COLUMBUS 05-C	450	12
COLUMBUS 07-E	439	12
COLUMBUS 17-C	437	7
COLUMBUS 25-G	402	9
COLUMBUS 07-A	317	14
COLUMBUS 13-A	263	16

The 72 precincts on this list registered the following results:

- A total of **45,308** votes for Barack Obama, and only 2,390 for Mitt Romney.
- An average vote of **629–33** per precinct, with Obama receiving **95%** of the vote.
- A margin of 42,918 votes in just these 72 precincts, which represents about 26% of Obama's total state margin of victory.

The voters in these 72 precincts only make up about 8.5% of the total vote in Franklin County, and about .86% of the total voting populace in Ohio. So, what you have here once again is a tiny portion of voters providing a massive margin for Obama. To be precise, in Franklin County:

About .86% of the state's voters provided Barack Obama with 26% of his winning margin in the state. When you combine these Franklin County precincts with the above precincts from Cuyahoga County, you have about 2.25% of the voters in the state giving Obama 71% of his total statewide margin.

Seems a little skewed, doesn't it? Is there any reason to believe that there might have been issues with the vote in Franklin County?

There were reports that hundreds of Tea Party members from the group True the Vote were denied access to serve as "observers" in dozens of polling places. They were denied access by the Franklin County Board of Elections allegedly due to a paperwork issue. The Board of Elections claimed that paperwork submitted by True the Vote was not properly filed, and thus the managers of those polling places were instructed not to honor any observers from the True the Vote group.

According to a story in the *Columbus Dispatch*, the observers from True the Vote were barred because while True the Vote did originally obtain signatures of support from at least five candidates for county office, in accordance with Ohio state law, that "at least most of the candidates who supported the organization's effort withdrew their backing."

These allegations were categorically denied by True the Vote President Catherine Engelbrecht, saying in a statement:

> *"These allegations by the Ohio Democratic Party are dangerous and offensive. The facts are simple: no citizen volunteer, including anyone else trained by True the Vote, took any action that was either illegal or unethical, particularly as it pertains to the placement of poll watchers. This is a final, desperate attempt to deny citizens their right to observe elections. The Ohio Democratic Party has projected paranoia on an international scale by promoting the idea that concerned citizens would dare observe elections to ensure a fair process."*

Do you believe it's just a coincidence that in places where Republican poll watchers were denied access or removed, that Obama received inordinately high percentages of the vote?

Next is Lucas County, situated in northwest Ohio, and within it you will find the city of Toledo and other cities such as Sylvania, Springfield, Waterville, and others. While there were no precincts with a zero for Romney, there were 16 in single digits, and 35 of them with over 94% of the vote. The actual vote in these 35 precincts, as reported on the Lucas County website is as follows:

Precinct	Obama	Romney	Margin	Obama
Toledo 8C	604	2	602	99.7%
Toledo 13C	473	2	471	99.6%
Toledo 14B	579	3	576	99.5%
Toledo 8F	698	4	694	99.4%
Toledo 8D	629	4	625	99.4%
Toledo 14C	606	4	602	99.3%
Toledo 13H	534	5	529	99.1%
Toledo 8B	622	6	616	99.0%
Toledo 10E	551	6	545	98.9%
Toledo 14F	543	6	537	98.9%
Toledo 14G	505	6	499	98.8%
Toledo 10D	488	6	482	98.8%
Toledo 13A	445	6	439	98.7%
Toledo 13E	397	7	390	98.3%
Toledo 14A	615	11	604	98.2%
Toledo 8H	652	15	637	97.8%
Toledo 10F	347	8	339	97.7%
Toledo 4F	424	11	413	97.5%
Toledo 14E	541	16	525	97.1%
Toledo 4J	351	11	340	97.0%
Toledo 6I	668	22	646	96.8%
Toledo 2I	239	8	231	96.8%
Toledo 13D	458	20	438	95.8%
Toledo 4H	406	18	388	95.8%
Toledo 14D	682	34	648	95.3%
Toledo 2H	337	17	320	95.2%

Toledo 6F	385	21	364	94.8%
Toledo 13G	635	35	600	94.8%
Toledo 15J	330	19	311	94.6%
Toledo 4G	503	30	473	94.4%
Toledo 4A	496	30	466	94.3%
Toledo 6H	642	39	603	94.3%
Toledo 6G	641	39	602	94.3%
Toledo 10C	456	28	428	94.2%
TOTALS	17791	513	17278	97.2%

The 35 precincts on this list registered the following results:

- A total of **17,791** votes for Barack Obama, and only 513 for Mitt Romney.
- An average vote of **508–15** per precinct, with Obama receiving **97.2%** of the vote.
- A margin of 17,278 votes in just these 72 precincts, which represents about 10.4% of Obama's total state margin of victory, delivered by .33% of the state's voters.

Once again, in a very small number of precincts, we see a huge margin for Barack Obama.

The final county we'll look at is Hamilton County, in southwest Ohio, which includes the city of Cincinnati. While Cuyahoga has always been a strongly Democratic area, Hamilton County is critical because for many years it had been solidly Republican.

Barack Obama won Hamilton County in 2008, and again in 2012 with 219,927 votes to Romney's 193,326, taking about 51% of the county's 418,894 votes and providing Obama a margin of 26,601 votes.

Just as we saw in Cuyahoga County, Franklin County, and Lucas County, the damage was done for Obama in a very small number of precincts and by a very tiny slice of the total electorate in the county. Following is a listing of the precincts that delivered the Obama margin in Hamilton County:

	Obama	Romney
CIN 2B	1062	59
CIN 3A	855	8
CIN 3D	1088	33
CIN 3E	991	31
CIN 7A	914	32
CIN 7B	447	4
CIN 7C	813	14
CIN 7D	929	25
CIN 7E	494	4
CIN 7F	681	7
CIN 7G	974	32
CIN 7H	1254	33
CIN 7I	1042	65
CIN 7J	392	13
CIN 8A	1045	49
CIN 9A	1113	20
CIN 9C	1058	35
CIN 10B	820	31
CIN 13A	1080	5
CIN 13C	1081	23
CIN 13D	1064	32
CIN 15C	703	4
CIN 15D	632	12
CIN 15J	561	12
CIN 17A	1270	15
CIN 18B	355	3
CIN 21B	934	61
CIN 22C	859	8
CIN23B	837	46
CIN 23E	808	19
CIN 24A	992	42
CIN 24H	336	1
CIN 24I	407	2
CIN 25A	1205	84
CIN 26D	1014	82
CIN 26E	1047	66
CIN 26H	455	2
LIN HT A	1058	2
LIN HT B	595	5

There are 39 precincts on this list, and the results they turned in were:

- A total of **33,265** votes for Barack Obama, and only 1,024 for Mitt Romney.
- An average vote of **853–26** per precinct, with Obama receiving **97%** of the vote.

- A margin of 32,241 votes in these 39 precincts representing about 19% of Obama's total state margin of victory.

It is factual to say that without these massive numbers in these precincts, Barack Obama would have lost Hamilton County. In fact, in the remaining precincts of Hamilton County, the vote was:

Mitt Romney	192,304 51%
Barack Obama	186,662 49%

So, in short, Romney won the rest of the county's 506 precincts, 93% of the precincts and 92% of the voters, by 5642 votes.

That was all undone in Hamilton County by margins that stretch the imagination in just 7% of the county's precincts. Again, just as we saw in other counties, a very tiny portion of the state electorate, about .6% of the state's voters, gave Obama a 26,601-vote margin in Hamilton County that helped him carry the state.

What has many people calling these results into question are the reports from several news services on election day that two precinct election judges were removed by the Hamilton County Director of Elections *for allowing unregistered voters to cast ballots.*

According to these reports, one of those precinct judges was removed from Precinct 13d, located at the Pentecostal Church in Cincinnati. It was alleged by a Romney/Ryan poll observer that people who were not registered were allowed to illegally "same day register," meaning they were told to sign the voter book, and then were given a regular ballot, not a provisional ballot. These people then voted and it was machine counted.

There is no way of knowing the exact number of people who were allowed to vote illegally, but reports placed the number at several dozen at a minimum. The Romney/Ryan poll observer protested about the illegal activities at the site and was ignored, then reported the violations to the Hamilton County Board of Elections, which apparently had received several reports of similar violations from other polling locations as well. Subsequently, the aforementioned precinct judge was eventually removed.

For the record, Obama won Precinct 13d by a total of 1064 - 32. And keep in mind, as stated above there were several other such reports from other precincts in Hamilton County as well.

How many other precincts were affected, which ones, and how many votes in all were illegally recorded?

Given that the local Board of Elections is run by a Democrat, these are all questions we will likely never have the answer to.

These weren't the only Democratic high jinks on Election Day. At least three people were charged for allegedly voting in Hamilton County in the 2012 election even though they are not Ohio residents.

Margaret Allen, 64, Ernestine Strickland, 84, and Andre Wilson, 49, were indicted in May 2013 on one count each of felony illegal voting. Allen was charged with attempting to vote by requesting an absentee voter ballot, despite being a resident of Florida and not living in Ohio since 2009. Strickland was charged with registering to vote and then voting early at the Board of Elections Office despite being a resident of Tennessee, not Ohio. Wilson was charged with registering to vote and then voting early at the Board of Elections Office using a fictitious address. According to board of elections officials, he lives in Northern Kentucky, but registered with an Ohio address and voted in Hamilton County.

In addition, Melowese Richardson, a Hamilton County poll worker plead no contest and was convicted on four counts of illegal voting, including voting three times for a relative who has been in a coma since 2003. A poll worker from 1998 until being fired this year, Richardson admitted she voted illegally in the 2008, 2011 and 2012 elections, and ironically it was her penmanship that led to her conviction.

"They noticed a bunch of absentee ballots coming from the same place with the same handwriting," Assistant Hamilton County Prosecutor Bill Anderson said. Other Board of Elections workers then recognized Richardson's handwriting.

Perhaps most sadly, a nun, Sister Marguerite Kloos, from Delhi Township in Cincinnati, was convicted of voting for a dead person, another nun who had passed away. Sister Kloos explained that she knew her deceased colleague would have voted that way. Oh.

As I stated above, a man by the name of Tim Burke serves as both the Board of Elections Chairman and also the Hamilton County Democratic Party Chairman. Am I the only one who sees that as sort of a conflict of interest?

To no one's surprise, when Mr. Burke was questioned about the multitude of incidents in his city, he said that there was no evidence of systemic fraud. He, as other Democrats typically do, stuck to the claim that these are simply isolated, misguided individuals, and that there certainly weren't enough votes affected to make a difference.

I would remind the conflicted Mr. Burke of a simple truth:

THESE ARE JUST THE ONES WHO WERE CAUGHT.

How many others were there? Everyone knew that Ohio was a key state, and you see above three examples of people from three other states that illegally snuck across the border and voted in Ohio.

How many others were there?

Officials were able to catch a stack of absentee ballots all signed by a poll worker named Melowese Richardson because someone happened to notice similar handwriting.

How many others were there?

A precinct judge in Precinct 13d allowed people to illegally "same day register," meaning they were told to sign the voter book, and then were given a regular ballot, not a provisional ballot. Dozens of these people then voted and it was machine counted.

How many others were there?

Prosecutor Joe Deters of Hamilton County summed up nicely why this is not only illegal but immoral:

"Our democracy is built on our lawful right to vote. Everyone's vote is weakened when some people decide to disobey the law."

Apparently, many Democrats don't feel that way.

In addition to issues on November 6, there were apparent issues with the vote in Cuyahoga and Hamilton counties even before Election Day. In a story reported by Newsmax on November 3, there were reports of possible fraudulent voter registrations in Hamilton County in Ohio. Election officials flagged 200 possibly fraudulent voter registration cards, including one voter who registered as "John Adolf Hitler." The suspected fraudulent registration for Mr. Hitler listed an address of 666 Heltz, Los Angeles.

Many and possibly all of the suspect voter registration cards in Hamilton County were filed by and organization called FieldWorks. These cards were flagged by the County Board of Elections as possibly being fraudulent. In addition, the Cuyahoga County Board of Elections reported three other Field-Works employees to the local prosecutor after finding what they said "appeared to be the same signature on multiple registrations." The fact that these incidents occurred in these two counties, Hamilton and Cuyahoga, that were so pivotal for the Obama campaign, is probably just a coincidence.

One last note on this topic. In the final week leading up to the election, whether planned or just another coincidence, 33,000 new voter registration cards were sent to county officials across the state of Ohio for verification. This late flood of registrations just added to the chaos.

When you add up all of the above results from Cuyahoga County, Franklin County, Lucas County and Hamilton County, you're talking about:

- Only 4 counties out of the 17 Obama carried.
- Only 8% - 10% of voters in those four counties.
- Only about 3% of the total electorate in the state.

And yet, this very small voting bloc provided Obama with such a huge number and high percentage of votes that these voters alone put him over the top.

When you add up the results for all the above precincts in these four counties, here's what they meant to Barack Obama and his victory in Ohio:

County	Precincts	In County	% of Vote	Voters for Obama
Cuyahoga	144	12%	**99.4%**	74,104
Franklin	72	8.5%	**95.0%**	42,918
Lucas	35	9%	**97.2%**	17,278
Hamilton	39	8%	**97.1%**	32,241
TOTAL	290		**97.4%**	**166,541**

I didn't include precinct level results for Summit County, Mahoning County, Trumbull County, or Lorain County. (Speaking of Lorain County, you may want to check out the swell pictures from Barack Obama's visit on the Lorain County website).

However, given what we've seen in the above four counties, it's reasonable to surmise that there were precincts in these four counties as well, and possibly in the other nine counties Obama carried in Ohio, that provided the same kind of results I've included here.

But even if there were no more results like this anywhere else in the state (unlikely as that is) the impact that just this small portion of voters had was staggering. Just focusing on the above information, all of the data straight from the various county and state websites, we can conclude the following:

- In these 290 precincts, representing roughly 3.2% of the voters in Ohio, there were 170,902 votes recorded for Barack Obama.
- In these 290 precincts, the 170,902 votes Barack Obama received were out of 175,281 recorded, which was good for **97.5%** of the vote. Obama received 51% of the vote in the state, *so this was nearly double.*
- More importantly, this small portion of voters, 3.2% of the state voting population, provided Obama with a margin of 166,541 votes.
- Given that Obama only won the state by 166,214 votes, *only 3.2% of the voters in Ohio provided 100.2% of Obama's winning statewide margin.*

In order to gauge what the above means, consider this:

THIS 3.2% of OHIO VOTERS, GAVE OBAMA **97.5 %** OF THEIR VOTES AND A MARGIN OF 166,541 VOTES. THE OTHER 97% OF THE STATE ELECTED MITT ROMNEY BY ABOUT 300 VOTES.

Again, keep in mind that we're only looking at 290 precincts, in four counties. If indeed this kind of turnout and these kinds of whopping margins and percentages were also turned in by other precincts in other counties as well, it becomes very apparent what kind of an uphill climb Mitt Romney was facing in Ohio on November 6.

It also becomes very fair to ask the question, are we sure the will of the people was carried out here?

Those who would criticize this analysis might say I also need to look at the most strident Republican precincts in Ohio. I did.

In Franklin County, the highest percentage Mitt Romney received in any precinct was 71.91%, and exactly 3 precincts were above 70%. In Hamilton County, the highest percentage for any precinct was 84%, with several being in the low 80% range. In Cuyahoga County, the highest percentage for Romney was 75%.

I've also taken a look at Warren County and Butler County, two very large counties in southern Ohio that Romney won with 70% and 63% of the vote, respectively. In Warren County, where Romney won by a tally of 76,561 to 32,909, there were a number of precincts that showed winning percentages in the '70s, but nothing remotely close to the astronomic 90+ percentages seen above.

In Butler County, Romney won by a tally of 105,176 to 62,388. There was one very small (13 votes) precinct where Romney won 12 of 13 for 92% of the vote, but there were no other precincts in the 90s. Only 5 precincts came in at 80% or above, 84 recorded 70% to 79%, and 112 precincts were at 60% to 69%. Of the 299 precincts in Butler County, Romney won 60%+ in 202 of them.

In these two counties, Mitt Romney won by a total of 181,737 to only 95,297, for 65.6% of the vote. These two counties had a combined winning margin for Romney of 86,440 votes, without anything resembling a zero voter turnout for Obama or 99.9% of the vote.

In none of these counties was there even a close equivalent in favor of Mitt Romney to what we saw for Obama. Nothing close to:

- The vote for Obama of 1064 – 32 from CIN 13D in Hamilton County (where the judge was dismissed for allowing illegal voting).
- The tallies like some in Cuyahoga County, where we saw votes of 637-0 in CLE 5E, 534-0 in CLE 5F, and 579-0 in CLE 2Q, and 515 – 0 in East CLE 4C.
- The ten precincts in Toledo that Obama won 6,344 to 42, or an average vote per precinct of 634 – 4, equating to 99.3% of the vote.
- And nothing to compare to votes in some of the Franklin County precincts, like COL 56D at 1312-34, COL 83C at 1040-57, and COL 83F coming in at 981-24.

All of the above information is indisputably, mathematically true, and anyone can find the same information at public websites. Simply put, if the above 290 precincts vote anywhere close to the state average, Romney wins Ohio in a landslide.

It is absolutely fair to say that Romney had much broader support across Ohio than did Obama. In fact:

- Not only did Mitt Romney win 71 out of 88 counties, he carried 36 of them, nearly half, with more than 60% of the vote.
- Romney carried a total of 13 counties with 66% or more of the vote.
- Of those, he carried 7 by more than 70%.

It would seem that what I was hearing leading up to and on Election Day was true, that Republicans across Ohio were energized and eager to vote for Mitt Romney. As I stated early in this chapter, if you take out 8 counties, Romney won the other 80 counties by about 435,900 votes.

But Obama was proclaimed the winner in Ohio. And the only way that could happen, as it turns out, was for Obama to receive incredible percentages of the vote, in massive numbers, somehow turned in throughout a small number of urban precincts. All of which are controlled by Democrats, where we saw poll workers turning in false absentee ballots, Republican poll watchers denied entry, reports of fraud by those poll watchers who weren't thrown out, Democrats sneaking across the border to vote illegally in Ohio, and many other examples of improprieties both before and on Election Day.

FLORIDA

Other than Ohio, the next most discussed state in the 2012 election was Florida. Barack Obama was declared the winner of the state of Florida by a very slim margin of 72,989 votes. Obama tallied 4,235,070 votes to Mitt Romney's 4,162,081. There are 67 counties in Florida, and Obama carried only 13. You can see which counties Obama carried on the map below, in light shade:

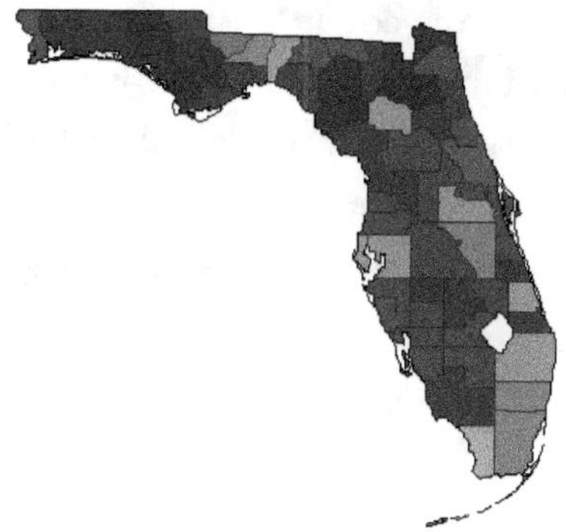

Just as we saw in Ohio, his victory margin was provided by a very small number of counties.

- Three counties, Miami-Dade, Broward, and Palm Beach counties provided Barack Obama with a combined margin of just over 574,000 votes.
- Six more counties – Hillsborough, Osceola, Orange, Pinellas, St. Lucie, and Leon - provided just over an additional 200,000 vote margin.

These nine counties, plus the four other smaller counties Obama carried, make up nearly one half of all Florida voters. Miami-Dade, Broward, and Palm Beach alone account for about 2.2 million and 26% of the voters in the state. Given the huge margins that Obama rang up in many of the 13 counties he carried, and the fact that he only won the state by 72,000 votes, the other 54 counties obviously went overwhelmingly for Mitt Romney.

Obama had margins of victory in four different counties—Miami-Dade, Palm Beach, Broward, and Orange—that were in excess of his 72,000-state-wide-vote margin. Any one of these could have provided him his margin of victory. However, I'm going to show you how Barack Obama received enough votes to build his 73,000-vote margin from two small pieces of just two counties.

Palm Beach County, located in south Florida, has 842 precincts. Barack Obama received 349,651 votes, about 58.5% of the vote, and 102,253 more votes than Mitt Romney. On the surface, this 58.5 percent of the vote that Obama garnered doesn't look too out of line, and in fact a significant number of precincts in the county went for Romney.

But like other Democrat-controlled areas we've looked at, it was again a tiny number of precincts in the county that delivered Obama both incredible numbers and more than ninety percent of the vote. Following is a listing of the key precincts that carried the day in Palm Beach County:

Precinct	Obama	Romney	Margin
6022	1091	43	1048
6024	1420	20	1400
7024	1387	20	1357
7026	1813	18	1795
7028	1459	67	1392
7040	1281	10	1271
7042	1408	9	1399
7044	1145	54	1091
7054	831	39	892
7058	1229	292	937

7060	1009	37	972
7064	1137	75	1062
7106	1463	30	1433
7128	1535	23	1512
7138	1211	259	952
7178	1410	213	1197
7180	1749	1121	637
7082	1099	11	1088
7186	1083	332	751
7196	1271	165	1106
7200	1180	54	1126
7210	1252	24	1128
7212	1059	110	949

In just these 23 precincts, out of 842 in Palm Beach County, Obama received 29,512 votes. Romney received just 2,107, meaning Obama took **93.6%** of the votes, and more importantly recorded a margin of **27,495** votes in this small piece of the county. The total number of votes cast in these 23 precincts was 31,529, *or about .38% of all votes cast statewide*. In other words:

The 27,495-vote margin that this tiny (.38%) portion of Florida voters provided Obama represents a huge chunk, _nearly 38%_, of his total 73,000 vote margin statewide. Nice symmetry, with .38% of the state's voters providing 38% of his statewide margin.

Actually, to say that these precincts helped Obama *carry the day* isn't entirely accurate, because much of the damage in Palm Beach County was done before the day even started. Obama held a huge lead of over 72,000 votes in Palm Beach County *before the polls even opened*. Remember, he only won *the entire state* by about 73,000 votes, and given some of the things you will read about what happened in early voting, it increases the belief that the eventual result was tainted.

Nearly half of his votes in Palm Beach County, _46%_, came in the form of Absentee and Early ballots. They provided him a commanding lead to start the day and 71% of his victory majority in the county when all the votes were counted. The numbers are as follows:

	Absentee	Early	Election Day	Total
Obama	74,466	86,582	188,150	349,158
Romney	51,549	37,414	158,290	247,253
Difference	22,917	49,168	29,860	101,945

In absentee ballots and in early voting, Obama received 64% of the vote, but on Election Day he got just 54%. What this means is hard to say, but how you view it likely has a lot to do with how you view absentee and early voting in general. Many people view them as a fertile ground to create votes, and as a means for a single voter to vote multiple times (which I will provide specific examples of). In any case, however these votes came to be, this is yet another case where a very small portion of voters provided what looks to be an unbelievable percentage of the vote.

Is it possible for .38% of voters in a state to *legitimately* provide 38% of a statewide margin? Or, could it possibly have been the result of, I don't know, maybe significant voting irregularities?

Before you answer, read the account below of some of the shenanigans that went on in early voting as reported by a Broward County poll watcher.

Broward County, also in south Florida, shows a total of 1,145,694 registered voters on their website, of which 52% are shown to be Democrats and about 22% Republicans. It will also be forever known as the "Home of the Hanging Chad." Broward was ground zero in Al Gore's attempt to somehow convince voters in 2000 that he actually won Florida and hence the presidency.

The overall results in Broward County, with all 778 precincts reporting, showed Barack Obama receiving 508,321 votes, about 67% of the vote, with 244,101 going for Romney. The same phenomenon played out here that we've seen elsewhere, with a small number of precincts giving Obama much higher percentages and absolutely incredible numbers of votes. I went through the list of just over one half of the precincts in Broward County, just under 400 of the A through N precincts, and found the following:

Precinct	Obama	Romney	Obama %	Margin
A015	1498	25	98	1474
A024	1239	62	95	1177
C006	1645	19	99	1626

C007	2053	87	96	1966
C016	1526	54	96	1472
C034	1981	24	99	1957
D007	1506	343	82	1163
D013	1326	222	81	1104
H002	1254	108	92	1146
H003	1341	120	92	1221
H005	1691	193	90	1558
H007	1202	196	86	1006
J013	1713	527	76	1186
J021	1608	657	72	951
K001	966	37	96	929
K002	978	33	96	945
K003	1124	43	96	1081
K006	1503	68	96	1435
K007	957	19	98	938
K010	1006	43	96	963
K011	1303	23	98	1280
K012	997	77	92	920
L004	911	29	97	882
L006	949	27	97	922
L007	1233	15	99	1218
L008	978	25	97	953
L009	1384	59	96	1325
L011	692	13	98	679
L012	1292	50	96	1242
L013	778	20	97	778
L015	1260	223	85	1037
L018	842	20	97	822
L022	1540	187	90	1353
L024	711	9	99	702
L025	1011	9	99	1002
L026	706	6	99	700
L027	1184	17	99	1167
L028	726	4	99	724
L029	1112	9	99	1103
M002	1014	50	95	964
M003	912	32	96	880
N001	1217	119	91	1098
N002	1265	138	90	1127
TOTAL	**52,134**	**3,958**	**93%**	**48,167**

These 42 precincts, about 5% of the precincts in the county, provided Obama with about 10% of his votes in the county. This .66% of the voters statewide also provided him with a 66% of his statewide margin.

Again, very nice symmetry, with .66% of the voters giving
Obama about 66% of his total margin in Florida.

When you add it up, in these two small pieces of Palm Beach County and Broward County, what you have is:

About 87,000 voters, or about 1% of the voters in the State of Florida, provided Obama with a margin of 75,662 votes. Again, he only won the state by about 73,000.

These two small pieces of Broward County and Palm Beach County combined to provide Barack Obama with over a 75,000-vote margin. If you *just took out the above 65 precincts* in these two counties, and left in every other result statewide, Mitt Romney wins the state of Florida. Said another way:

About 99% of the voters of Florida cast about 2600 more
votes for Mitt Romney than for Barack Obama

As I mentioned above, and to absolutely no one's surprise in the Land of The Hanging Chad, we heard numerous reports of suspected voter fraud in Broward County. Everyone has heard the line "vote early and often," but in south Florida it doesn't exactly appear to be a joke.

Diane Sori, a poll watcher during several days of early voting, said she observed multiple cases of voter irregularities. One of the most prominent was witnessing individuals not being signed in at the voter station in order to verify that no earlier votes had been cast. In Florida, the law clearly requires that each voter's license or voter ID card be "swiped" prior to the voter being allowed into the voting booth. Mrs. Sori signed affidavits with election officials swearing that she saw numerous individuals who did not sign into their voting stations but were still allowed to vote.

She went on to detail other infractions, such as situations where an individual's signature failed to match their voter data, and were then asked for address information to verify their identity. If the voter didn't know their address, or gave incorrect information, Mrs. Sori testified that she actually saw poll workers *turn the computer screen towards the person* so that they could verify the address, *essentially providing it to them*. This is clearly against voter laws in Florida.

Mrs. Sori also stated that she witnessed:

- People voting more than once. She said that she recognized many individuals who after voting early in the day, came back for a second round of voting later that same day. In one specific instance, Sori stopped a repeat voter and confronted the polling site manager. In that case, the individual did admit he'd voted earlier in the day and was asked to leave.

- Busloads of individuals being brought in from other areas of Broward County outside of the precinct.

- In instances where a voter had no ID, or if there was some problem with their license, these people would be sent to the site manager's station. Ostensibly, this is where evidence of positive identification was required for them to be cleared to vote. She testified that apparently these people were cleared and allowed to vote based on information exchanged on a *telephone call*, sight unseen. How do you identify yourself on a phone call?

- In spite of very clear rules disallowing same day voter registration and voting, she testified that the site manager at her polling station repeatedly allowed both registration and voting on the very same day.

Mrs. Sori and a fellow poll watcher testified that they witnessed these and other instances of voter fraud with incredible frequency, in numbers she could not even estimate, throughout her three days observing early voting in Broward County.

What about on Election Day? It probably won't surprise you that even though Mrs. Sori was given "emergency status" that morning, she was never allowed on the premises, so she was not able to observe what went on or to monitor for voter fraud on Election Day. As you will see, that happened in other states as well.

There were hundreds of precincts in Palm Beach County, Miami-Dade County, Orange County, Pinellas County, and Hillsborough County that I didn't examine. Given what we have seen in other Democratic controlled counties, I think it's safe to assume a potential for similar activities and illegal voting in those counties and precincts as well. If this is what happened in the precincts in Palm Beach and Broward counties that we did look at, why would you assume otherwise in those we did not?

There were many other examples of fraud in Florida. In February, 2013, in Pompano Beach, a woman who is a convicted felon was accused of voting illegally in the November 2012 election. Onakia Lanet Griffin, 33, was charged with submitting false voter registration information, false swearing and fraud in casting a vote. Apparently, she had an "I Vote Early" bumper sticker that gave her away. Good thinking.

In May of 2013, a top staffer for Florida Democratic Rep. Joe Garcia resigned after being implicated in a voting-fraud scheme. Chief of Staff Jeffrey Garcia resigned after taking responsibility for the plot. Rep. Garcia referred to it as a "well-intentioned attempt to maximize voter turnout," going on to say that the system is "prone to fraud."

That must explain why just a few hours before the resignation, law-enforcement investigators raided the homes of Giancarlo Sopo, the congressman's communications director, and John Estes, his 2012 campaign manager. The investigation centered around a sophisticated scheme to manipulate last year's primary elections by submitting hundreds of fraudulent absentee-ballot requests.

Garcia won the primary and later defeated incumbent Republican David Rivera in the general election. I have to believe that in both cases he won because of a "well-intentioned attempt to maximize voter turnout."

There were a number of reports regarding issues in St. Lucie County, where Allen West was running for reelection. There were original reports that more votes were cast than there were registered voters, when the board listed the total number of votes cast as 247,383. Given that they only list 175,554 registered voters it justifiably raised some eyebrows, as this would have placed voter turnout at 140.92%.

That controversy was dismissed by some when it was revealed that the ballot in St. Lucie County was a two-page card, and there were only about 124,000 votes cast. However, the St. Lucie County board of elections admitted to problems with electronic voter machines, at least in the congressional race.

It was reported that on the night of the election, *4,000 votes were flipped from incumbent Congressman Allen West to his Democrat challenger.* Simply put, the flipping of those votes would have changed the results of the election, as Allen West lost his district by less than 2,500 votes. Election officials admitted that the 4,000 votes had initially been read incorrectly.

I want to repeat that:

West lost by less than 2,500 votes. There were reports that 4,000 votes were flipped on election night from West to his opponent, to which officials admitted at least some error.

To date, there has NEVER been a full accounting of what happened.

In addition, there were also reports that 799 votes were double counted in this tight congressional race, and that one precinct with 7 registered voters somehow recorded about 900 votes. I wonder if 7 registered voters somehow casting 900 votes also qualifies as a "well-intentioned attempt to maximize voter turnout." I have a feeling that in Democratic precincts, it does.

After a series of adjustments, West's opponent held a lead of 1,907 votes in a race with about 330,000 votes cast, just barely (another coincidence?) above the .5% that automatically triggers an automatic recount of all votes. The board of elections agreed to a "partial recount," and some early votes were recounted. Votes cast on days 6–8 were recounted, but not votes cast on days 1–5. There were never any answers as to why.

Congressman West and the Republican Party asked repeatedly for a full recount as well as a count of all voter signatures. Eventually, after stonewalling by the St. Lucie County officials, Allen West simply gave up. Again, there has never been a complete review of the irregularities in this election or of the final vote count.

This does beg a question in a close state like Florida:

> If machines can "flip" vote from Allen West to his challenger, can they not somehow flip votes from Mitt Romney to Barack Obama as well?

Again, all of the results you see above you can look up for yourself. A tiny portion of the state's electorate, less than 1% of the voters, accounted for Obama's winning margin. Votes were double counted, votes were apparently flipped, there were fraudulent absentee ballot requests, people were allowed to register and vote same day illegally, people were seen and even caught voting more than once, felons voted illegally, busloads of voters were seen coming into precincts in Broward County, and Democratic staffers were forced to resign.

PENNSYLVANIA

Barack Obama won the state of Pennsylvania by 309,840 votes, out of nearly 5.7 million reported. Obama collected 2,990,274 votes to Mitt Romney's 2,680,434, or about 52.08% of the vote. Compared to Romney's 46.68%, a casual observer may conclude that Obama won handily in Pennsylvania.

Not so. Just as we saw in Pennsylvania and Florida, the vast majority of counties in Pennsylvania went for Romney. Of the 67 counties in Pennsylvania, Obama carried only 13, ironically just as we saw in Florida, and as shown in light shade on the map below:

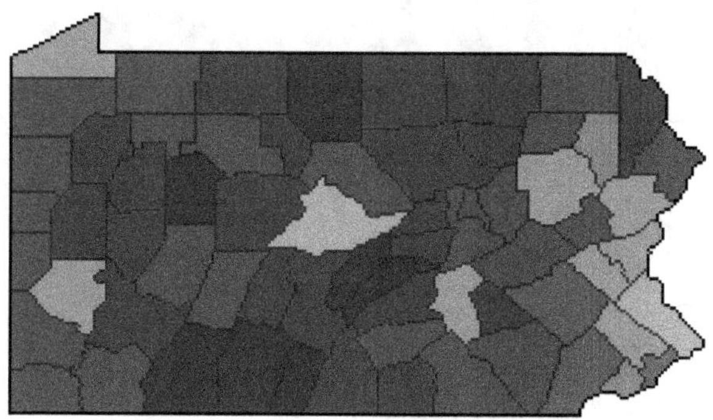

Even though Obama won 13 counties In Pennsylvania, the election really came down to just one, Philadelphia County.

When you take a look at the other twelve Pennsylvania counties that Obama carried, the victory margins were much less decisive and more in line with the rest of the country. Obama carried Delaware County with 60% of the vote, while Erie, Allegheny, Montgomery, Lackawanna, and Monroe all gave him just over 55%. Certainly, all solid wins, but the total combined margin Obama had over Romney in the twelve counties he carried other than Philadelphia was roughly 300,000 votes.

Given that Obama only won the state by about 309,000 votes, he may have been in trouble were it not for the City of Brotherly Love.

Philadelphia County, encompassing the city of Philadelphia, gave Barack Obama all the votes he needed and more to carry the Keystone State. The turnout and margins Obama garnered in many of the Divisions and Wards within the city were not only incredible but also dramatically different than those seen anywhere else in the state.

There are 66 Wards in Philadelphia County, over 1600 divisions, and some of the Wards that did the very best for Barack Obama are as follows:

Ward	Votes	Margin	% of Votes
40	17,802	16,934	95.2%
34	17,656	16,973	96.0%
50	15,317	15,149	98.7%
36	12,929	12,417	95.6%
10	12,724	12,585	98.7%
22	12,524	12,215	96.9%
52	11,810	11,315	95.6%
61	11,511	10,845	94.2%
49	11,351	11,148	98.1%
51	10,524	10,430	98.8%
17	11,430	11,290	98.6%
12	10,295	10,099	97.6%
13	9,762	9,657	98.8%
46	9,800	9,547	96.0%
59	10,274	10,083	97.7%
60	8,683	8,852	98.6%
3	9,647	9,594	99.3%
4	9,955	9,900	99.3%
5	13,301	10,423	80.0%
6	6,516	6,449	98.7%
7	6,770	6,452	95.3%
11	6,681	6,636	99.2%
16	5,226	5,176	98.9%
28	5,920	5,886	99.4%
37	6,455	6,351`	98.2%
38	8,099	7,378	91.4%
42	9,598	9,043	94.3%
44	6,633	6,575	98.9%

48	7,285	6,581	90.8%
32	9,146	8,921	97.1%
43	8,362	8,136	97.2%
33	6,814	6,078	90.0%
35	10,268	8,620	85.7%

In these 33 Wards, one half of the 66 Wards in Philadelphia County:

- Barack Obama received 331,068 votes, *96% of the vote*, and won by a margin of 317,738. There were 59 districts where Romney didn't receive a single vote.
- This one half of this one county therefore *gave Obama his entire margin of victory in the state of Pennsylvania*, and provided him with more margin than the other twelve counties he carried *combined.*

When all was said and done, the totals for all of Philadelphia County were that Barack Obama received **588,806 votes to just 94,467** for Mitt Romney. We also saw:

- An average vote per ward of **8,921 for Obama to 1,431 for Romney,** or 86% of the vote.
- A margin for Obama of **494,339 votes,** which represented *160% of his winning margin in the state.*

In other words, the other 66 counties of Pennsylvania, including the other twelve counties carried by Obama, elected Romney by a margin of 184,499 votes, or about 3.2%.

What makes these results in Philadelphia County even more suspicious was the fact that early on the morning of November 6 many Divisions in Philadelphia literally *threw out* their Republican poll watchers. This was documented to have happened in at least the following Divisions:

Ward 32, Div 13
Ward 43, Div 14
Ward 56, Div 1
Ward 56, Div 22
Ward 32, Div 28

Ward 32, Div 28
Ward 12, Div 17
Ward 39, Div 1
Ward 24, Div 9
Ward 18, Div 25
Ward 43, Div 14
Ward 29, Div 18
Ward 65, Div 19
Ward 20, Div 1
Ward 6, Div 11

You can go on-line and listen to what took place in Philadelphia's 20th Ward, 1st Division, when the woman "in charge" of that division refused to allow in the court-appointed Republican minority inspectors, stopping them from doing their job and monitoring the vote. You will hear her say very clearly, "I do not care what the law says."

In another of these Divisions, it was reported that a female inspector was literally "physically thrown out."

Why they were thrown out, and what happened while they were gone, is all speculation. What we do know is that it took hours for a court order to get the poll watchers reinstated, and that you will find many of the Wards in question *just happen to show up* on the above list of Obama's best Wards, registering over 95% of the vote. As stated above, there were 59 districts where Romney got ZERO votes, just as we saw in Cuyahoga County.

I read, though I was not been able to confirm, that the vote in these 59 districts was 19,605 for Obama, to ZERO for Romney. Given that we were able to confirm a vote for Obama in 144 precincts in Cuyahoga County of 74,566 to 453, it doesn't seem unrealistic.

Let me rephrase that. It does seem unrealistic, unbelievable, and impossible. What I meant is that it's certainly right in line with what happened in other Democratic controlled precincts we reviewed in Ohio and Florida where there were also reported improprieties.

Even Larry Sabato, a longtime Democratic pollster, expressed surprise in the numbers:

"I'd be surprised if there weren't a handful of precincts that didn't

Maybe some of this could have been avoided. A law was passed in Pennsylvania that mandated use of a photo ID in all future elections, but a ruling by a Pennsylvania judge on October 2 decreed that while election officials could ask voters for a photo ID, they could not require one. While a lack of photo IDs may help explain massive turnout, it would not in any way explain away zero votes in 59 precincts or the kinds of margins seen above.

It is also important to note that in the other districts in Philadelphia, *voter turnout was only about 60%*. However, in these districts where poll watchers were removed, *turnout was over 90%*, and Obama received over *99% of the vote*. Since no one was there to watch, and since these wards are controlled by Democrats, we'll never know whether poll watchers being removed had anything to do with either the massive turnout or the incredible margins.

We're also unsure what impact murals of Obama on the walls of polling places may have had.

Once again, as we saw in Ohio and Florida, a small subset of the vote, about 6% of the total vote in Pennsylvania, made the difference. Poll watchers were denied access or physically removed, and in many of those divisions there were no votes for Romney, voter turn-out was dramatically higher in these divisions than in other parts of the city, and basically one half of one county provided the entire state's margin of victory.

VIRGINIA

There were 1,971,820 votes recorded for Barack Obama in Virginia, 51.2% of the vote, versus 1,822,522 votes cast for Mitt romney. Obama's margin of victory was 149,298 votes out of the nearly 4 million recorded, or about 3.7% of the recorded vote.

Virginia has a rather unique form of local and county government, as the Commonwealth is divided in to 95 counties and 39 "independent cities." As the name implies these cities are completely independent from and not part of any county, and a few examples of such independent cities are Hampton, Norfolk, Richmond, and Portsmouth. What makes this even more confusing is that several counties and cities have the exact same name, including Bedford, Fairfax, Franklin, Richmond, and Roanoke. Norfolk and Alexandria are two that used to share the same name, but those counties changed their names presumably to end some of the confusion. To make matters worse, having similar names doesn't necessarily mean that these counties and cities are close geographically. Richmond County isn't anywhere near Richmond City, and Franklin County is even farther from the City of Franklin. I'm glad we've cleared that up.

Obama carried only 19 of the 95 counties, but did much better in the independent cities, winning 28 of the 39. The map below shows cities and counties carried by Obama, in light shade:

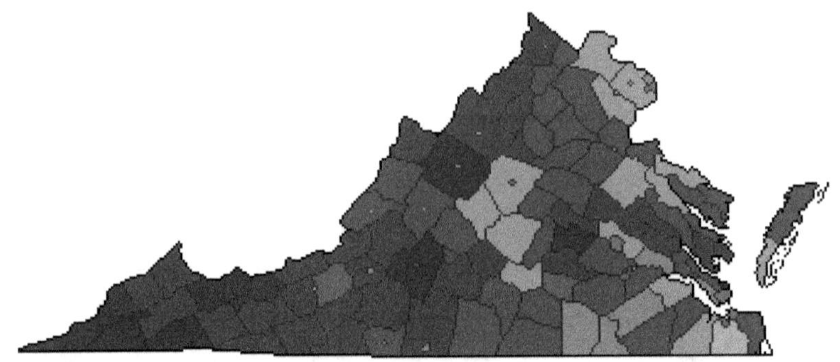

Of the 18 counties carried by Obama, none gave him more than 70% of the vote. The highest percentage he showed in any county was 69.1% in Arlington County. Charles City County was at 66%, and five others, including Fairfax County, were at 60% to 63%, with the rest between 51% and 57%.

Mitt Romney had very strong support throughout most of the counties and many of the cities of Virginia, winning 77 of the 95 counties and 11 of the 39 cities. *This means that Mitt Romney won 66% of the individual voting municipalities.* Not only did he carry these areas, but in many cases, he carried them with substantial margins. In fact, Romney received:

- *Over 70%* of the vote in 10 counties and in one city.
- *Over 65%* of the vote in 16 more counties and 3 more cities.
- Over 60% of the vote in an additional 15 counties and another city.
- Over 55% of the vote in 10 more counties.

When you add it up, 30 counties and cities gave Mitt Romney more than 65% of the vote, and 46 of them gave him more than 60% of the vote.

It was only in a few counties, and primarily in the "independent cities" that Obama really made hay. While Obama lost 81% of the counties, he won 72 % of the independent cities. In the end, he carried the state of Virginia by recording very large margins in:

- The Washington DC area. The three large northern counties near DC, Fairfax County (+108,500), Arlington County (+46,795), and Prince William County (+28,873) combined to give him 184,168 more votes than they cast for Mitt Romney.

Alexandria City provided another 31,950-vote margin, for a total from the DC area of a 216,118-vote advantage for Obama.

The DC area accounted for nearly 150% of Obama's state-wide margin. Thank God for government workers.

- Richmond City, which provided him with 78% of the vote and a margin of 55,871 votes, and   the southeastern port cities of Norfolk City, Hampton City, Portsmouth City, and Newport News City all registered more than 70% of the vote for Barack Obama, and gave him an additional 111,379 vote margin.
- The vote totals for Obama in these nine counties and cities, and the margins they provided for him, are as follows:

	Obama	Romney	Margin	% of Margin
FAIRFAX COUNTY	315273	206773	108500	73%
RICHMOND CITY	75921	20050	55871	37%
ARLINGTON COUNTY	81269	34474	46795	31%
NORFOLK CITY	62687	23147	39540	26%
ALEXANDRIA CITY	52199	20249	31950	21%
PRINCE WILLIAM COUNTY	103331	74458	28873	19%
HAMPTON CITY	46966	18640	28326	19%
NEWPORT NEWS CITY	51100	27230	23870	16%
PORTSMOUTH CITY	32501	12858	19643	13%
	821247	437879	383368	257%

The above nine counties and cities gave Barack Obama:

- A total of 821,247 votes, or 42% of his total votes in the state.
- A total of 65% of the vote, and a margin of 383,368, or about 257% of his total statewide margin of 149,298.

In other words:

The other 125 counties and cities in Virginia gave Mitt Romney *nearly a quarter of a million more votes, 234,120* to be exact, than they gave Barack Obama. Said another way, Romney won the rest of the state by 6%.

And just as we've seen in Ohio, Florida, and Pennsylvania, not only was it a small group of counties and cities that made the difference, it was only a small group of precincts in those areas that led the way.

Looking first at the counties to the north and Alexandria City, we don't see margins like the "99%–100%" we saw for Obama in other areas. In Alexandria City, there were really 10 precincts out of 27 that went heavily for Obama, but none exhibited the incredible levels we saw elsewhere.

The top 10 precincts for Obama in Alexandria City all cast between 76% and 83% of the vote for Obama, with an average of 79%, as follows:

Alexandria City Precincts	Obama	Romney	Margin	% Obama
306- WILLIAM RAMSAY SCHOOL	2127	425	1702	83%
305- JOHN ADAMS SCHOOL	2077	455	1622	82%
302- PATRICK HENRY REC CENTER	1579	372	1207	81%
304- SAMUEL TUCKER SCHOOL	2273	547	1726	81%
106- CORA KELLY CENTER	2144	537	1607	80%
303- CHARLES E BEATLEY LIBRARY	1671	436	1235	79%
108 – G WASHINGTON MDDL SCHOOL	1846	549	1297	77%
209- JAMES K POLK SCHOOL	2014	607	1407	77%
107- MT VERNON RECREATION	2049	622	1427	77%
307- SOUTH PORT	1466	465	1001	76%
	19246	5015	14231	79%

The same can be said for Fairfax County. Though the county delivered a huge margin of about 100,000 votes, there were only 3 in excess of 80%, but there were 55 others with between 66% and 79% of the vote going to Obama. These are certainly very strong margins, but nothing like Cuyahoga County or Broward County.

Richmond City, however, and a few of the other independent cities, provided a far different story.

The percentages Obama received in many precincts in Richmond City, and the sheer numbers of votes, is positively overwhelming. These precinct-by-precinct results for Richmond City, pulled right from the Virginia.gov website, are as follows:

Richmond City Precincts	Obama	Romney	Margin	Obama
602- SIX HUNDRED TWO	1272	7	1265	99%
802- EIGHT HUNDRED TWO	1094	8	1086	99%
701- SEVEN HUNDRED ONE	1439	11	1428	99%
310- THREE HUNDRED TEN	737	7	730	99%
610- SIX HUNDRED TEN	1186	23	1163	98%
304- THREE HUNDRED FOUR	1165	24	1141	98%
604- SIX HUNDRED FOUR	914	19	895	98%
603- SIX HUNDRED THREE	998	22	976	98%
702- SEVEN HUNDRED TWO	1106	27	1079	98%
606- SIX HUNDRED SIX	1426	35	1391	98%
301- THREE HUNDRED ONE	963	33	930	97%
911- NINE HUNDRED ELEVEN	1195	53	1142	96%
305- THREE HUNDRED FIVE	1098	49	1049	96%
811- EIGHT HUNDRED ELEVEN	1367	63	1304	96%
509- FIVE HUNDRED NINE	1314	62	1252	95%
306- THREE HUNDRED SIX	969	46	923	95%
814- EIGHT HUNDRED FOURTEEN	1004	48	956	95%
303- THREE HUNDRED THREE	748	36	712	95%
703- SEVEN HUNDRED THREE	945	48	897	95%
806- EIGHT HUNDRED SIX	1516	100	1416	94%
908- NINE HUNDRED EIGHT	964	64	900	94%
706- SEVEN HUNDRED SIX	1735	121	1614	93%
902- NINE HUNDRED TWO	600	43	557	93%

510- FIVE HUNDRED TEN	1476	108	1368	93%
213- TWO HUNDRED THIRTEEN	1845	142	1703	93%
909- NINE HUNDRED NINE	1486	128	1358	92%
910- NINE HUNDRED TEN	1282	120	1162	91%
810- EIGHT HUNDRED TEN	1132	109	1023	91%
903- NINE HUNDRED THREE	1459	141	1318	91%
302- THREE HUNDRED TWO	916	94	822	91%
609- SIX HUNDRED NINE	825	99	726	89%
705- SEVEN HUNDRED FIVE	785	100	685	89%
812- EIGHT HUNDRED TWELVE	1609	229	1380	88%
503- FIVE HUNDRED THREE	1239	179	1060	87%
505- FIVE HUNDRED FIVE	1073	162	911	87%
504- FIVE HUNDRED FOUR	1710	261	1449	87%
206- TWO HUNDRED SIX	1732	288	1444	86%
501- FIVE HUNDRED ONE	1378	295	1083	82%
508- FIVE HUNDRED EIGHT	675	175	500	79%
307- THREE HUNDRED SEVEN	872	269	603	76%
203- TWO HUNDRED THREE	1029	328	701	76%
412- FOUR HUNDRED TWELVE	629	202	427	76%
708- SEVEN HUNDRED EIGHT	1113	359	754	76%
404- FOUR HUNDRED FOUR	1389	449	940	76%
308- THREE HUNDRED EIGHT	996	330	666	75%
607- SIX HUNDRED SEVEN	671	227	444	75%
113- ONE HUNDRED THIRTEEN	1082	396	686	73%
114- ONE HUNDRED FOURTEEN	1277	656	712	69%
208- TWO HUNDRED EIGHT	1178	540	638	69%
204- TWO HUNDRED FOUR	1115	530	585	68%
410- FOUR HUNDRED TEN	1002	491	511	67%
207- TWO HUNDRED SEVEN	1112	588	524	65%

402- FOUR HUNDRED TWO	1300	805	495	62%
309- THREE HUNDRED NINE	516	409	107	56%
413- FOUR HUNDRED THIRTEEN	761	624	137	55%
414- FOUR HUNDRED FOURTEEN	864	754	110	53%
111- ONE HUNDRED ELEVEN	681	614	67	53%
409- FOUR HUNDRED NINE	1233	1118	115	52%
112- ONE HUNDRED TWELVE	504	470	34	52%
105- ONE HUNDRED FIVE	639	679	-40	48%
101- ONE HUNDRED ONE	929	1049	-120	47%
102- ONE HUNDRED TWO	415	553	-138	43%
104- ONE HUNDRED FOUR	520	968	-448	35%
106- ONE HUNDRED SIX	374	1161	-787	24%
##Central Absentee	4428	849	3579	84%
#Provisional	107	18	89	86%
TOTALS	**74707**	**19285**	**55422**	**79%**

In Richmond City:

- 10 precincts recorded 98% or more of their votes for Obama, giving him a margin of 11,154 in just those ten precincts. To put that in perspective, those 11,154 votes represent 7.5% of Obama's total margin statewide, *yet the voters in these 10 precincts only represent .3% of the vote in the state.*

- The top 30 precincts for Obama in Richmond City gave him 91% of the vote or more. These 30 precincts gave Obama an incredible 95% of the vote, and a margin of 33,560 votes.

    These 33,560 votes provided Barack Obama 22% of his winning margin in the commonwealth of Virginia, *cast by only .97% of the voters.*

We saw similar results in other independent cities. Next up are some of the precincts from Norfolk City:

Norfolk City Precincts	Obama	Romney	Margin	% for Obama
414- YOUNG PARK	1875	13	1862	99%
403- BRAMBLETON	1051	8	1043	99%
402- BERKLEY	1373	16	1357	99%
411- HUNTON Y	590	7	583	99%
313- UNION CHAPEL	823	12	811	99%
404- CAMPOSTELLA	1561	27	1534	98%
405- CHESTERFIELD	1640	29	1611	98%
303- BOWLING PARK	1880	38	1842	98%
212- PARK PLACE	1284	35	1249	97%
310- ROSEMONT	2370	72	2298	97%
306- LINDENWOOD	1024	70	954	94%
301- BALLENTINE	1596	131	1465	92%
207- LAMBERT'S POINT	1873	171	1702	92%
412- INGLESIDE	1311	172	1139	88%
104- TITUSTOWN	787	111	676	88%
TOTALS	**21038**	**912**	**20126**	**96%**

The above shows 15 of the 51 precincts in Norfolk City, with all 15 giving Obama more than 88% of the vote, a total of 96%, and a margin of 20,216 votes. These 20,126 votes gave Barack Obama a full 13.5% of his winning margin in Virginia, cast by only .57% of the voters.

The next city is Petersburg City, and though small it was mighty for Obama. There are only eight precincts, but they delivered in total over 90% of the vote, as follows:

Petersburg City Precincts	Obama	Romney	Margin	% for Obama
101- FIRST WARD FIRST PRECINCT	1380	125	1255	92%
201- SECOND WARD FIRST PRECINCT	1920	200	1720	91%
301- THIRD WARD FIRST PRECINCT	1809	428	1381	81%
401- FOURTH WARD FIRST PRECINCT	1557	209	1348	88%

	Obama	Romney	Margin	Obama
501- FIFTH WARD FIRST PRECINCT	1733	88	1645	95%
601- SIXTH WARD FIRST PRECINCT	1640	32	1608	98%
701- SEVENTH WARD FIRST PRECINCT	1781	124	1657	93%
##Central Absentee	2457	320	2137	88%
#Provisional	6	1	5	86%
TOTALS	**14283**	**1527**	**12756**	**90%**

This small voting bloc gave Barack Obama an additional 12,756 vote margin, and these voters, only .42% of the voters in the state, gave Obama 8.5% of his total statewide margin.

The last city we'll look at is Portsmouth City, and specifically we'll examine just eight precincts:

Portsmouth City Precincts	Obama	Romney	Margin	Obama
011- ELEVEN	1100	6	1094	99%
021- TWENTY-ONE	877	7	870	99%
013- THIRTEEN	1029	9	1020	99%
027- TWENTY-SEVEN	1321	14	1307	99%
026- TWENTY-SIX	1318	15	1303	99%
005 – FIVE	1079	13	1066	99%
014- FOURTEEN	1249	22	1227	98%
028 – TWENTY-EIGHT	<u>1658</u>	<u>33</u>	<u>1625</u>	<u>98%</u>
TOTALS	9631	119	9512	99%

In these eight precincts, Obama received roughly 99% of the vote, and a whopping 9,512 vote margin out of 9,750 cast. The average vote in these 8 precincts was Obama 1204 – Romney 15.

This small slice of the Virginia electorate, about .25%, delivered 6.4% of Barack Obama's victory margin in the Commonwealth of Virginia.

Portsmouth City is yet another microcosm of how Barack Obama won this election. A small number of urban precincts delivered a ridiculous percentage of the vote, in excess of 99%, and did so in very high numbers, allowing Obama to offset solid margins by Mitt Romney in a large majority of the overall precincts and counties.

When you add the above Portsmouth City results to the three portions of Richmond City, Norfolk City, and Petersburg City, you have a total of only 51 precincts, only 2.5% of the state's voters, delivering a margin of 75,964 votes for Obama, or almost 51% of his margin statewide.

Should it be possible for 51 precincts, 2% of the precincts in Virginia, about 2.5% of the voters, to account for more than one half of a candidate's winning margin?

These counties and cities in Virginia also revealed another interesting and common phenomenon. Barack Obama registered very strong results in "absentee" ballots in virtually every city and county, getting a higher percentage of those votes than elsewhere in that municipality. For example:

- In Richmond City, Obama won the absentee vote by 4428 – 849, 84% of the vote compared to 79% in the county overall, and a margin of 3,579 votes.
- In Hampton City Obama won 72% of the overall vote, but won 84% of the absentees, good for a margin of 3,426 votes.
- In Portsmouth City, Obama received 82% of the absentee ballots, compared to 72% overall, and providing him with a 2,725-voter margin.
- In Fairfax County, the percentage of the absentee ballots was 64%, with the total county at 59.7%. The margin Obama had in absentee ballots alone in Fairfax County was 10,777 votes.

Absentee ballots *alone* in Richmond City, Hampton City, Portsmouth City, and Fairfax County accounted for a 20,507-vote margin for Obama, 13.7% of his state margin.

Is there any reason to believe fraud may have been committed in Virginia?

In April 2013, the Virginia attorney general's office announced that it was investigating "several possible cases of duplicate voting" uncovered after a comparison of the commonwealth's registration rolls against voter lists in 21 other states.

Nikki Sheridan, spokeswoman for the State Board of Elections, said the board requested the investigation, prompted by the results of a voter registration database check that turned up more than 308,000 duplicate registrations in Virginia. Of those, ***more than 97,000 were listed as having voted in recent elections in Virginia.***

> Wait a minute. Don't Democrats always tell us that fraudulent registrations don't *really* mean that anyone is actually showing up and voting illegally?

While it's true that some of these duplicate registrations could be explained by a person moving to a different state, attending college or serving in the military, given that we have proof of Democrats sneaking across borders and voting illegally in other states, this is absolutely a cause for concern. It's also true that one of the oldest Democratic tricks in the book is to have out-of-state college students register and vote both at school and in their home state.

In 2012, Virginia passed a law requiring voters to present identification to cast a ballot, although the ID did not have to include a photograph. In 2013, Gov. Robert F. McDonnell (R) signed new legislation that will require Virginians to show a photo ID before casting a ballot.

Dara Fox, a poll watcher in Woodbridge, Virginia, in Prince William County, gave a detailed account on a telephone call to WMAL in Virginia (which can be heard on the Internet), of the following examples of, in her words, "rampant voter fraud":

- Many people who came in and said that the name on their ID was wrong or other information was inaccurate because they were recently divorced, had moved, or for some other reason.
- Many voters who could not provide their correct address when signing in. She also said she was shocked to see Democratic poll workers "helping out" voters in remembering their address.
- There were a number of voters whose ID had, for example, an Asian name, while the person voting clearly was not Asian.
- Many people, when asked to provide their correct address, said they could not do so because they did not speak English, and were allowed to vote anyway.
- Several voters presented with an age on their ID that was radically different than what they appeared to be. She specifically referred to an ID with an age of 42, when the person looked to be about 18.

- She was very upset when on multiple occasions, when she went to check people off to show that they'd voted, *she found that that voter had already been checked off.* When asked how many times this happened, she said at least "30–40 times," just that she saw.
- She stated that she was absolutely certain that she saw a great number of people voting more than once, and also specifically heard the same names more than once. Again, she said that she saw and heard these things more times than she could keep up with.
- She also said she saw "busloads" of people coming in at once, and that part of the problem in trying to monitor what was going on was that the lines were long, that they were overwhelmed, and that they'd been specifically told that they should not engage voters in conversation.

Mrs. Fox made it very clear that the things she saw were not just a few isolated incidents, but rather were things that she witnessed dozens and dozens of times, and that they went on all throughout the day. She also reported that she had heard from other poll watchers in Virginia who told her that they'd seen the exact same things.

After hearing Mrs. Fox's account of what she saw, there were a number of calls and e-mails to the station from other poll watchers in Virginia who reported seeing the exact same things that she'd seen in the precincts in which they'd worked.

If the above examples don't convince you that voter fraud was a significant part of the Obama win in Virginia, you could take the word of this son of a Democratic Congressman.

Meet Patrick Moran. Patrick is the son of Virginia Democratic Congressman James Moran. You can go on-line and listen to him talk with an undercover reporter about the best and most effective ways to commit voter fraud. You will hear the son of this Democratic Virginia congressman talk on video with an undercover reporter about how to forge documents in what Moran thought was a discussion with a sympathetic voter who wanted to engage in illegal voting efforts to reelect Obama.

The video is by Project Veritas, the organization headed up by James O'Keefe whose undercover videos also thankfully helped bring down ACORN and more recently led to the firing of an Obama campaign worker engaged in apparent voter fraud in Houston. The younger Mr. Moran can be heard on the video encouraging the reporter to create phony utility bills that would allow the casting of multiple votes in the November 6 election. In case you're wondering, yes, soliciting fraudulent voter registrations and fraudulent ballots is a federal crime.

In the video you will hear Moran, who works in an office shared with other Democratic campaigns including the president's reelection organization, say and do the following:

- Offer advice on circumventing Virginia election law. He is heard to say, "Realistically speaking what do you need to vote for … if you were to go in and vote for someone else in Virginia, you go to the polling place, you need a utility bill."
- When challenged that a utility bill is "going to be kind of hard to get," Moran replies that possibly something less than that would work, possibly just "a name and an address, which I think would probably be easy."
- Moran goes on to say that fraudulent voters could rely on the help of friendly, sympathetic, and motivated Democratic poll watchers. He says, "You'll have somebody in house that, if they feel that what you have is legitimate, they'll argue for you."

I doubt you'll be shocked that in January of 2013, Arlington County Police decided not to bring charges against young Mr. Moran. It was not reported whether or not being the son of old Mr. Moran had anything to do with that.

Once again, in Virginia, we saw the same theme play out as in other states. Strong majorities for Mitt Romney in most of the counties of a state, but those results being undone by ridiculous margins and percentages in a small number of precincts, with even bigger margins on a curiously large number of absentee ballots. Three hundred thousand voters were found to have duplicate registrations, and about one hundred thousand of them voted in recent elections. We heard from poll workers who described "rampant voter fraud," examples of people who didn't know their address until it was provided to them by Democratic poll workers, voters who clearly are not the person on the ID they present, voters who show up multiple times in a day, votes cast under a name where the book showed that that person had already voted, and a Democratic Congressman's son seen on tape giving a tutorial on how to commit voter fraud.

NEVADA

Nevada was described at various points during the election as a battleground state, but many people assumed it would go for Obama. It ultimately did, with Obama receiving 531,373 votes to 463,567 for Mitt Romney, per the Secretary of State's website. This gave Obama a winning margin in the state of 67,806 votes, or about 6.8%. While this margin may seem impressive, what we see once again is just a small portion of the state going for Obama, as shown on the map below in light shade:

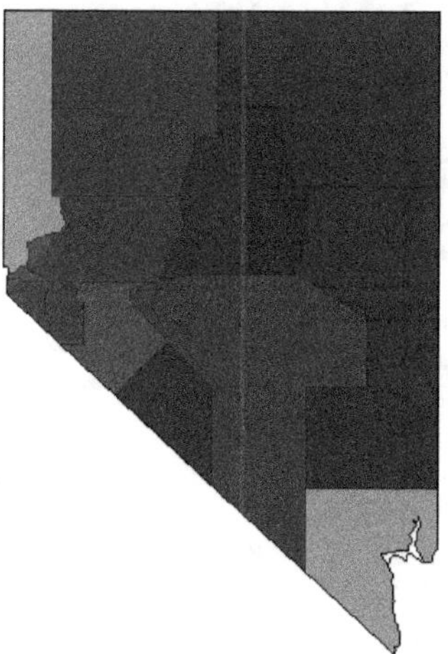

There are only sixteen counties in Nevada, plus Carson City, and as we've seen in many other states most went solidly for Mitt Romney. Romney carried fourteen counties and Carson City, Obama only two. It was no surprise that the county that really delivered the state for Obama was the spiritual home of the SEIU, Clark County. Clark County gave Barack Obama a total of 389,936 votes, to 289,053 for Romney, a margin of 100,883. Given that Obama only won the state by 67,806, this would represent about 150% of Obama's winning margin. Said another way, the other fifteen counties in Nevada, plus Carson City elected Mitt Romney by about 33,000 votes, or by about 3.3% of the vote.

Not only did Romney win fourteen counties in Nevada and Carson City, but he won them in many cases overwhelmingly. When comparing the head-to-head vote, Mitt Romney carried about 86% in Eureka County, 81% in Lincoln County, more than 70% in five others, and more than 60% in five more.

That's twelve counties with more than 60% of the vote, and seven of them with more than 70%. Washhoe County was the only other county Obama won, and he only received about 51% of the total vote there and a margin of 6,956 votes out of about 184,000 cast.

Here's what the 16 counties of Nevada and Carson City look in terms of the vote for Obama or Romney:

County/City	Obama	Romney	Margin	% for Romney
Eureka	107	663	-556	86%
Lincoln	400	1,691	-1,291	81%
Esmeralda	92	317	-225	78%
Elko	3,511	12,014	-8,503	77%
Lander	534	1,580	-1,046	75%
White Pine	983	2,601	-1,618	73%
Churchill	2,961	7,061	-4,100	70%
Humboldt	1,737	3,810	-2,073	69%
Pershing	632	1,167	-535	65%
Lyon	7,380	13,520	-6,140	65%
Douglas	9,297	16,276	-6,979	64%
Nye	6,320	10,566	-4,246	63%
Storey	920	1,321	-401	59%

Mineral	863	1,080	-217	56%
Carson City	10,291	12,394	-2,103	55%
Washoe	95,409	88,453	**6,956**	48%
Clark	389,936	289,053	**100,883**	43%
Total State	531,373	463,567	67,806	

Not exactly a landslide for Obama. In fact, once again it's accurate to say that Mitt Romney had much more widespread support in this state than did Obama.

In reviewing the precinct results in Clark County, there wasn't the type of incredible high nineties percentages such as we saw in precincts in Ohio, Pennsylvania, Florida, and other states. There was some with very high numbers, and percentages, a few of which were:

Precinct	Obama	Romney
4310	707	6
4028	728	9
4017	819	12
4616	998	22
4597	816	81
4552	977	74
4527	927	88
4528	967	23
4507	951	100
4461	913	33
4306	1087	199
5581	<u>692</u>	<u>94</u>
	10,585	941

In just these twelve precincts, Obama received 10,585 votes out of 11,526 cast, or about 92% of the vote, and a margin of 9,644. These voters would represent about 1% of the total vote in the state, and they provided nearly 10% of Obama's total margin for the state. There were dozens of other precincts in Clark County where Obama commanded large numbers of votes and large margins, ultimately carrying him to his 100,000-vote margin from this one county.

What's very interesting about the vote in Nevada is the incredible number of votes that took place before November 6. This is shown in the chart below, direct from the Secretary of State's website:

2012 General Election Total State

Active Registered Voters	1,258,409	
Election Day Turnout	311,613	(24.76%)
Early Turnout	619,381	(49.21%)
Absentee Turnout	85,670	(6.80%)
Total Turnout	1,016,664	**(80.77%)**

As you can see, **61%** of 1.016 million votes cast were recorded before Election Day. Only **31%** were cast on Election Day. Therefore, twice as many votes came in the form or early votes as did on November 6. Clark County looked very similar, and clearly was the driver of the state results:

2012 General Election Clark County

Active Registered Voters	852,413	
Election Day Turnout	205,693	(24.13%)
Early Turnout	436,568	(51.21%)
Absentee Turnout	50,001	(5.86%)
Total Turnout	692,262	(81.2%)

In Clark County, **63%** of 692,262 votes cast were recorded before and only **30%** were cast on Election Day. Again, twice as many votes came in before November 6. In both the state and Clark County, turnout was above 80%.

How you feel about that likely depends on whether or not you believe early voting provides additional opportunities for duplicate voting or other mischief. Those who argue in favor of such early voting would point to the high 81% turnout as a positive, while other may question whether this number is inflated by votes that are not authentic, or perhaps people who vote both before and on Election Day.

Was the Nevada vote totally legit? There is certainly past history that raises doubt.

In May 2009, two ACORN officials, Christopher Edwards and Amy Buse-fink, were indicted on charges of criminal voter registration fraud in Nevada.

This was in connection with their activities leading up to the 2008 Presidential Election. These charges were brought based on an investigation by the Nevada Secretary of State's office.

Their investigation concluded that of the total of 91,002 voter registration forms submitted by ACORN in Clark County, only 25.6% (23,186 forms) were "related to valid persons."

In other words, about 75% were bogus.

In addition, ACORN was also charged with paying their canvassers cash bonuses if they returned more than 21 complete forms, also illegal under Nevada law, because such bonuses encourage submission of fraudulent forms.

Acorn itself was also is named in the criminal complaint, because according to the Secretary of State's office, Acorn's training manuals "clearly detail, condone and . . . require illegal acts, such as requiring its workers to meet strict voter-registration targets to keep their jobs."

On August 19, 2009, Christopher Edwards plead guilty to reduced charges and agreed to testify against ACORN and the other individual charged in the case. Edwards gave testimony in September 2009 that during the 2008 election, he did pay registration workers a $5 bonus if they turned in 21 or more voter registration cards in a day.

We can go back to the 2004 election as well. Nevada was considered a swing state in that election. George W. Bush won in Nevada, beating John Kerry by just 21,500 votes. Prior to the election, there were a number of reported incidents involving voter registration fraud, with our friends at ACORN again at the center of it.

At that time, fraudulent voter registration forms were so pervasive that in July of that year the Clark County Registrar of Voters, Larry Lomax, referred the matter to the FBI for criminal investigation. The Registrar of Voters subsequently turned the matter over to the Nevada Department of Investigations, prompting President Bush to comment on his concerns about voter registration during a visit to Nevada in September of that year.

But no discussion of voter fraud in Nevada would be complete without mentioning Senator Harry Reid and his friends at the SEIU.

In 2010, Reid defeated his Republican challenger Sharron Angle by a 50.2% - 44.6% margin. It was speculated by many that his victory was in large part the doing of his friends in the Service Employees International Union. According to critics, voting machines in Clark County, where about three-fourths of Nevada's voters reside, were programmed to place a check mark next to Harry Reid's name before anyone ever voted.

County officials insisted that nothing of the sort occurred, but their denial is suspect given that one of Harry Reid's sons, Rory Reid, is county commission chairman. In addition, lending further credence to the belief that not everything was on the up and up: A collective bargaining agreement between Clark County and SEIU Local 1107 *put the union in charge of servicing all voting machines.* You read that right. The SEIU, unabashed and notorious supporters of the Democratic Party, was appointed per the agreement to service all voting machines in Clark County.

Since we know that SEIU Local 1107 technicians service Clark County voting machines, I think we can assume that they would then be responsible for any issues or potential glitches that may have occurred. During early balloting in late October, a number of voters in Boulder City (near Las Vegas) came forward with the above-mentioned complaints that Reid's name had already been checked. These were by no means isolated incidents, as there were reportedly a very large number of such complaints in Clark County.

Democrats, naturally, dismissed these as resulting from sensitive touch screens. That's possible, but if that were the case, why were all the reports benefitting Harry Reid, and none of these very sensitive touch screen "malfunctioning" with votes for his opponent?

What makes Reid's victory by nearly 6 points all the more suspicious is that he had been well behind in the polls. Four Rasmussen polls showed Angle ahead of Reid, and two weeks before the election she led by a margin of 50% to 47%. If anything, the momentum was in her favor, as a week later she'd increased her lead to 4 points, 49%-45%.

And yet, somehow, we are asked to believe that in the space of a week, Harry Reid gained a full 10 points, going from what was projected as a 4% defeat to a 6% victory.

Remember that this was 2010, an election that saw sweeping Republican gains all over the country. In that environment, what in any election would be highly improbable becomes something that can only be called what it was—a stolen election.

As to Reid's son Rory serving as chairman of the Clark County board of commissioners and helping old Dad with his race, Democrats are quick to point out that Rory was the Democratic nominee in the 2010 gubernatorial race, and lost big to Republican Brian Sandoval. They argue that if Rory were capable of rigging his father's victory, he would certainly have done the same in his own race.

Nice try. Rory was behind in the polls by more than 20 points, and Sandoval only wound up defeating him by about 12%, 53.4% to 41.6%. Mathematically speaking, the net gain in the final week of the election comparing the final polling to the actual vote was about 10% in both races. While this was enough to snatch victory for Harry, it wasn't enough for Rory to salvage his race. The SEIU apparently can only do so much.

Unfortunately, even if there were an investigation, it would be very difficult to prove any of this. Computerized voting leaves no audit trail to see who voted for which candidate. State voting officials in Nevada, as in many states, have a habit of removing memory cards and hard drives not long after the polls close, thus eliminating evidence of voter intent. There are federal laws that require retention of "all records and papers" for 22 months, related to everything from application, registration, payment of poll tax, or any other actions requisite to voting. With Democrats controlling the election boards in so many states, you can imagine that their adherence to these statutes, or their willingness to investigate, is less than zealous.

As I stated above, putting the SEIU in charge of voting machines in akin to putting the foxes in charge of the henhouse. There are numerous examples of how overt and extremely aggressive the SEIU was in 2012 in their support of Obama, and one such example took place shortly before the election in Bedford, OH, a suburb of Cleveland. Mitt Romney was campaigning in Bedford, and given that Bedford is not a wealthy town, Democrats were hoping to put together a large protest to embarrass the Republican candidate. Unfortunately for them, there turned out to be far more Romney fans in the small community than they expected, and they were having trouble putting together enough people for a respectable protest.

To make sure that there were enough people protesting Romney's visit, the SEIU came to the rescue, and hired a number of union people, *paying them $11 an hour and bussing them in to Bedford* to masquerade as real Bedford citizens against Romney. When a few of the protestors spoke to reporters and admitted as much, others in the group quickly surrounded them and got them away from the cameras.

Another example of the SEIU's willingness to do whatever it takes to support Democrats, up to and including breaking the law, took place in Wisconsin during the closely contested April 2011 election for a Wisconsin Supreme Court seat.

An SEIU official named Clarence S. Haynes voted in the election despite the small detail that he was not a resident of the state of Wisconsin. According to October, 2012 affidavit filed by the Milwaukee County District Attorney's office, Haynes, whose actually resides in Clearwater, Florida, voted along with two other SEIU organizers in Glendale, Wisconsin on April 5, 2011. They provided the address of a Residence Inn as their Wisconsin address.

It was later revealed that as many as 50 SEIU employees lived at the hotel leading up that election, and that the SEIU spent $146,000 to keep them there. I wonder how many of those other forty some people also voted illegally in that election? And here's a much bigger question:

Do you think maybe the SEIU also paid for hotel stays and illegal votes during the 2012 election in key swing states?

Focusing back on Nevada, with regard to the Senate race in Nevada in 2010, what we have is:

- The SEIU Local 1107, which supports Harry Reid, had control of the voting machines in Clark County.
- Members of the SEIU have demonstrated that they are not above breaking the law to support candidates they favor.
- Many voters in 2010 claimed that Senator Harry Reid's name was automatically checked off on the ballot when they went to vote.
- Rory Reid, Harry Reid's son, is chairman of the Clark County Commission, which would be responsible for conducting any investigation into any wrong doing in Clark County elections.
- Harry Reid miraculously gained 10 points over the final week of the election to hold onto his seat.

That's how Harry Reid won in 2010, and it's certainly possible that it's also how Obama won Nevada in 2012.

Apparently, Harry, his son, and Barack Obama are disciples of a famous Russian philosopher by the name of Josef Stalin. Stalin once said:

"Those who cast the votes decide nothing.
Those who count the votes decide everything."

Oregon

I think if you asked most people, they'd say that Oregon is a state that overwhelmingly supported Barack Obama. Most would say that the citizens of Oregon, almost universally, applaud his polocies and voted for his reelection. I actually thought that was the case myself until I started looking into it. The mostly **dark** map below, which illustrates the number of counties that voted for Mitt Romney, tells a very different story. In fact, this looks a lot like Ohio. And Florida. And Pennsylvania. And Virginia. And Nevada.

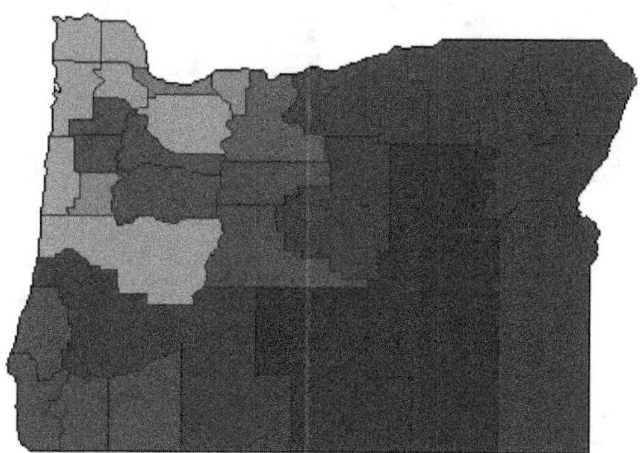

As I began to examine the actual county-by-county election results in Oregon, I was shocked at just how many counties voted for Mitt Romney, and in fact how many did so by large margins.

Obama won the state by a total of 970,488 votes to 754,175, garnering 56.3% to Mitt Romney's 43.7%, and had a margin of victory of 216,313 votes. This would lead many to argue that Oregonians did indeed vote overwhelmingly for Obama.

However, when you look closer, it's not as clear cut as some would have you believe. Below is a listing of all of the counties in Oregon, and their election results, direct from the Oregon Secretary of State's web site:

County	Obama	Romney
Baker	2,369	5,702
Benton	27,776	14,991
Clackamas	95,493	88,592
Clatsop	9,861	7,249
Columbia	12,004	10,772
Coos	12,845	14,673
Crook	3,104	6,790
Curry	4,625	6,598
Deschutes	36,961	42,463
Douglas	17,145	30,776
Gilliam	371	639
Grant	853	2,926
Harney	832	2,607
Hood River	6,058	3,429
Jackson	44,468	49,020
Jefferson	3,301	4,642
Josephine	14,953	23,673
Klamath	8,302	18,898
Lake	770	2,808
Lane	102,652	62,509
Lincoln	13,401	8,686
Linn	20,378	28,944
Malheur	2,759	6,851
Marion	56,376	60,190
Morrow	1,202	2,532

Multnomah	274,887	75,302
Polk	16,292	17,819
Sherman	319	678
Tillamook	6,293	5,684
Umatilla	8,584	15,499
Union	3,973	7,636
Wallowa	1,253	2,804
Wasco	5,211	5,229
Washington	135,291	93,974
Wheeler	266	545
Yamhill	19,260	22,045
Total	**970,488**	**754,175**

Of the 33 counties in Oregon, Barack Obama won only 10. He won one county by more than 70%, Multnomah County, the largest in the state, with 78% of the vote.

He won four others—Benton, Hood River, Lane, and Lincoln—with 61% to 65% of the vote, and won five others with between 53% and 59% of the vote.

Barack Obama lost 23 of the 33 counties in Oregon, and in many cases lost them overwhelmingly. Mitt Romney carried:

- **5** counties with more than 70% of the vote.
- **11** more counties with 61%–69% of the vote.
- **7** more counties with 50%–59% of the vote.

Mitt Romney received more than 66% of the votes in 12 counties, versus only two for Obama. Mitt Romney carried more counties with over 60% of the vote in Oregon (16) that Barack Obama carried period (10). And not all the counties Romney won were small counties where people cling to their guns and bibles. Romney won in Marion, Jackson, Deschutes, Linn, and Josephine counties, and lost by only 7,000 votes in Clackamas County.

Unfortunately for Mitt Romney, the results show that in the very largest counties in the state:

- Obama won 78% of the 350,189 votes recorded in Multnomah County, bringing him 274,887 votes and a whopping margin of 199,585 votes. This gave him 92% of his margin statewide.
- Obama also won 59% of the vote in Washington County, good for 135,291 votes and a margin of 41,317.
- Obama claimed 62% of the vote in Lane County, worth 102,652 votes and 40,143 more than were cast for Mitt Romney.

Three counties, 512,830 votes, 53% of his total vote in the state, and a w hopping margin of 281,045 votes. Given that Obama won the state by 216,313, these three counties gave him 130% of his statewide winning margin. In other words:

MITT ROMNEY WON THE OTHER 30 COUNTIES BY 64,732 VOTES, OR BY ABOUT 3.8% OF THE STATE VOTE

When you look at Multnomah County, what (again) drove that county to a 78% share for Obama was an incredible turnout and performance in a small number of precincts where he got more than 90% of the vote. A listing of some of these precincts is as follows:

Precinct	Obama	Romney	Margin	% for Obama
4303	3,549	134	3,415	96%
4302	3,656	166	3,490	96%
4311	2,833	154	2,679	95%
4310	3,619	198	3,421	95%
4207	3,624	200	3,424	95%
4304	3,729	210	3,519	95%
4203	3,048	175	2,873	95%
4201	3,278	189	3,089	95%
4204	3,759	265	3,494	93%
4301	3,637	265	3,372	93%
4208	3,186	239	2,947	93%
4206	3,657	282	3,375	93%
4205	3,747	301	3,446	93%

4306	3,539	359	3,180	91%
4308	3,567	370	3,197	91%
4305	3,500	365	3,135	91%
3301	3,348	354	2,994	90%
4401	2,821	332	2,489	89%
4503	3,195	381	2,814	89%
4209	3,329	429	2,900	89%
4210	3,235	451	2,784	88%
4307	3,407	491	2,916	87%
4401	3,137	458	2,679	87%
4504	3,573	531	3,042	87%
4401	3,137	483	2,654	87%
4401	3,217	496	2,721	87%
4211	3,349	543	2,806	86%
4603	3,525	580	2,945	86%
TOTALS	95,201	9,401	85,800	91%

In just 28 precincts in Multnomah County, Barack Obama received:

- **95,201** votes, to only 9,401 for Mitt Romney, **91%** of the vote.
- An average vote tally and margin per precinct of *3400 – 336*.
- An **85,800**-vote margin, about **40%** of his margin in the total state, delivered by about 6% of the state's voters.

As you review the above list, look at how *strikingly similar* the number of votes for Obama, the number of votes for Romney, and the resulting margins are. Does this look suspicious, or at least odd to anyone else?

All but two of these precincts are plus or minus 400 votes versus the average of 3400 votes for Obama. It could cause a cynical person to theorize that these precincts all had a "targeted" number of votes, or a "quota," that they needed to reach. *And it appears that this quota would have been a 3000-vote margin per precinct.*

For the record, the average margin in these precincts was 2959 votes.

Romney actually did pretty well in a number of precincts in Multnomah

County, but the percentages and sheer numbers in the above very large precincts created an incredible number of votes to overcome. The same can be said for just a few precincts in Lane County, as follows:

Precinct	Obama	Romney	Margin	Obama %
1123	1366	143	1223	91%
1125	2616	276	2340	90%
1127	2202	199	2003	92%
1129	2448	518	1930	83%
1131	2631	333	2298	89%
1133	2397	524	1873	82%
1135	2802	562	2240	83%
1345	3009	474	2535	86%
1347	2174	253	1921	90%
1349	838	109	729	88%
1783	<u>1888</u>	<u>186</u>	<u>1702</u>	<u>91%</u>
	24371	**3577**	**20794**	**87%**

In just 11 precincts in Lane County, the tally for Obama was:

- 24,371 votes, an average of 2216 per precinct, 87% of the vote. In these same precincts, Mitt Romney received an average of 325 votes.
- An 20,794-vote margin, over half his margin in the county, and yet it was delivered by only 11 out of 91 precincts, and by only about 16% of the voters in the county.

While Washington County delivered a lot of votes (135,291) votes and a big margin (41,317) for Obama, there wasn't the kind of high 90s percentages for him that we saw above and in other states. There were a few precincts with 100% for Obama, but they were small. Washington County also had a huge turnout, 82% of the voters came out, and there were 50 out of the 160 precincts that gave Obama solid but not spectacular results. Those precincts are as follows:

Precinct	Obama	Romney	Margin	Obama
352	454	106	348	81%
391	199	55	144	78%
393	401	125	276	76%
361	896	313	583	74%
384	1514	529	985	74%
378	1046	373	673	74%
401	1079	394	685	73%
381	400	149	251	73%
387	410	154	256	73%
333	1697	679	1018	71%
366	1204	489	715	71%
353	1124	462	662	71%
383	820	339	481	71%
306	324	138	186	70%
407	981	434	547	69%
350	1597	716	881	69%
359	1049	490	559	68%
355	1592	772	820	67%
399	1204	601	603	67%
382	1575	793	782	67%
363	1793	915	878	66%
379	1795	924	871	66%
446	1991	1027	964	66%
319	542	286	256	65%
386	1611	854	757	65%
349	1237	658	579	65%
331	1144	609	535	65%
375	158	85	73	65%

400	1430	771	659	65%
385	1642	888	754	65%
360	1361	740	621	65%
344	1922	1049	873	65%
309	2258	1238	1020	65%
362	1959	1075	884	65%
351	1135	638	497	64%
358	925	524	401	64%
406	1532	873	659	64%
371	1176	692	484	63%
417	608	360	248	63%
372	925	553	372	63%
332	1057	633	424	63%
354	1993	1195	798	63%
368	1932	1247	685	61%
364	2264	1491	773	60%
389	1175	775	400	60%
409	1251	828	423	60%
390	1839	1245	594	60%
323	1336	908	428	60%
380	1149	782	367	60%
405	2197	1499	698	59%
TOTALS	62903	33473	29430	65%

These 50 precincts gave Obama 65% of the vote, not drastically more than the 57% for the entire county, but they gave him huge numbers of votes. They did contribute nearly half of his votes in the county, and over 71% of his margin.

As I mentioned above, the turnout in many of these counties was huge, well above the national norm. One possible reason for that may be that Oregon doesn't have an Election Day so much as they have an "Election Season."

Starting on September 26, it lasts about 6 weeks, roughly the same as Lent. As anyone who's ever had to give up something for Lent can tell you, Lent lasts a long time.

When the sun came up on Election Day, nearly 58% of the voters in Multnomah County had already voted. Their 82.45% turnout is well above normal. This six-week voting cycle also produced turnout in Lane County of 81%, and 82% in Washington County.

The question is, do you believe it's legitimate?

There is one story from Oregon I want to tell you about. A man from Bend, Oregon, by the name of Aaron Hirschman was convicted for offering $20 on Craig's list in an ad that was headlined "Want to make an easy $20 for voting?" The ad went on to say that anyone interested could meet him outside the county elections office in Bend, and that "All you need to do is bring your UNFILLED clean voting ballot and let us fill it out then you sign, then we hand it to the volunteer in the voting booth. It's that simple! Then you get $20. We'll be there all weekend through Tuesday."

If you're thinking that it's a stretch to include this story as an example of rampant voter fraud, that's a fair argument. You could absolutely argue that this is as much an example of stupidity as it is voter fraud, but I've included this story for a different reason.

I think there's something else at play here besides just stupidity. While this individual is certainly an idiot, I suspect this could be an illustration of something far more important.

I believe there's a pervasive feeling among liberals, at least many of them, that their cause is so good, that their leaders so righteous, that even breaking the law is tolerable, so long as they triumph. In short, I don't think these people see what they're doing as voter fraud so much as they see it as "vote creation." Their creation of votes, authentic or not, is in their mind's justified by their belief that theirs is the cause of justice. That seems to be the mindset of many Liberals, and I would absolutely include the current occupant of the White House in that number. Their outlook is that "the end justifies the means," therefore whatever means they must employ to achieve their end is completely justified.

When you look at Oregon, you see a state where Mitt Romney again carried far more counties than Obama, and in many cases by large margins. Romney got more than two thirds of the vote in about half the counties in the state. You see results from three counties that went for Obama with inordinately

high turnout numbers, all above 81%, and you also see strikingly if not unbelievably similar numbers of votes from precinct to precinct in Multnomah
County. In many of those precincts Obama won by an average of 3400 votes
to only about 400, and when you look at the list provided above it is eerie, and
frankly unbelievable, that so many precincts could look so virtually identical.

Where have we seen this before?

The most famous case of a Presidential election featuring alleged fraud was the 1960 race between Richard Nixon and John F. Kennedy. The race was incredibly close, in fact Kennedy received only about 113,000 more votes than Nixon out of about 68 million cast. Kennedy won the electoral vote 303-219, but many states were very close and could have gone either way. Illinois and Texas are the two most talked about, but California was also closely contested, first being declared for Kennedy before absentee ballots gave the state to Nixon on November 17.

Even before Election Day, rumors circulated about potential fraud in Chicago, where Mayor Richard Dailey and his machine were notorious for delivering huge Democratic margins and turnouts. When all was said and done, Kennedy won Cook County, which of course includes Chicago, *by 450,000 votes*. He won the state of Illinois *by only 9,000 votes*. Below is a map showing the Illinois county by county results in 1960. The counties that went for Kennedy are light, those that went for Nixon are dark.

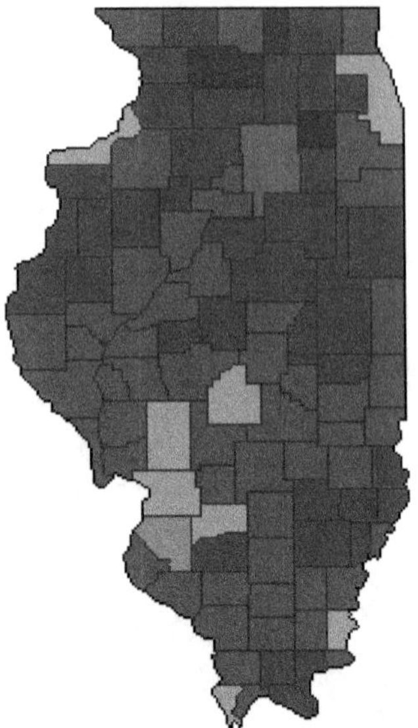

In short, a gigantic margin in urban areas—in Chicago, near St. Louis, and near the Quad Cities—offset the vast majority of counties and voters in other parts of the state and gave Kennedy the win.

Déjà vu all over again? I would suggest that it's not a coincidence that another politician who happens to hail from Chicago would win the presidency in a similar manner in 2012.

If we look at the above map from Illinois in 1960, then look at the below maps from the 2012 election of the six states we've just reviewed, it's impossible not to see that they look very similar:

Ohio   Pennsylvania

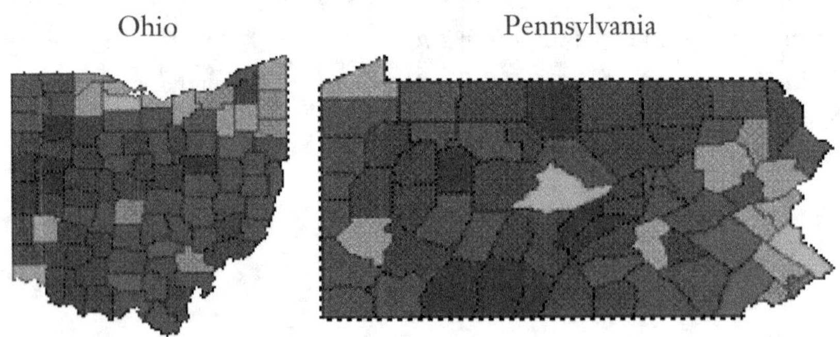

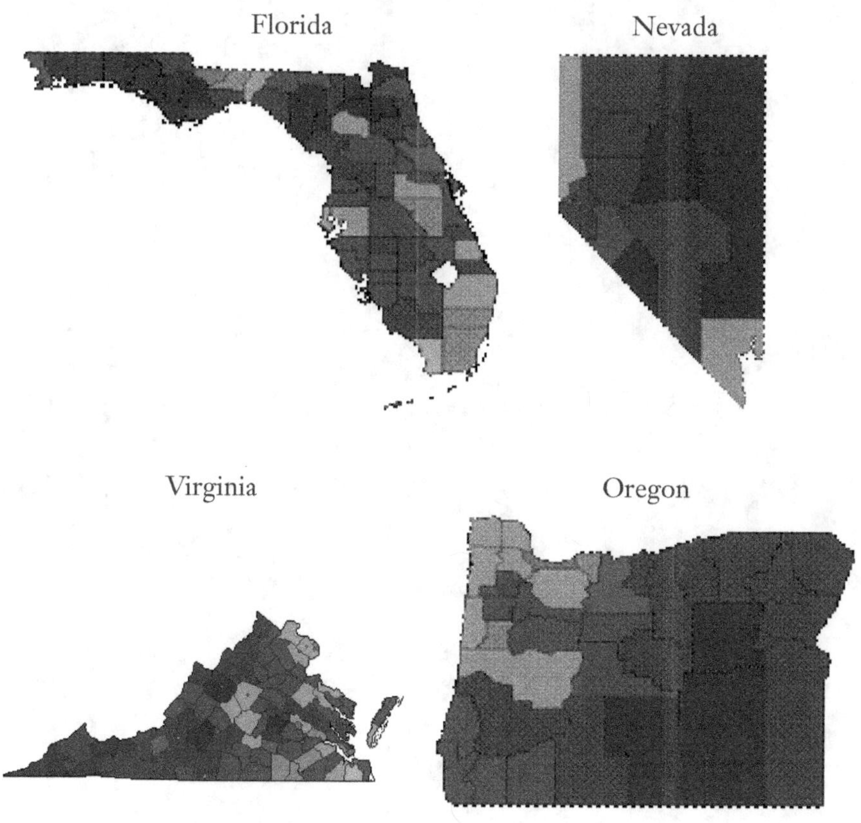

And what's worse, we've shown in our county-by-county analysis that only a small number of precincts and voters in the small numbers of counties Obama won are what made the difference—just as it was in 1960. Allegations of voter fraud didn't begin with the 1960 election, but it's the election most people think of when discussing voter fraud in a presidential election. Chicago was at the center of it in 1960, and in 2012 it appears that one of its sons relied on that playbook again.

The Old Democratic Playbook

The tried-and-true formula that Democrats have relied on forever in their fabrication of votes is really a simple one, as shown earlier:

1. Get as many "registered voters" as possible on the voter rolls, legitimate or otherwise.
2. Ensure that these "registered voters," legitimate or otherwise, living or dead, are never removed from the voter rolls.
3. Ensure that someone shows up on election day (or before, or both) and votes under the names of all of those "registered voters," legitimate or otherwise.
4. Fight against requirement of a photo ID, or any other potential roadblocks that may interfere with their manufacturing of votes.
5. Label anyone who makes any attempt to reduce voter fraud as nothing more than a racist.

When it comes to voter fraud, rule number one for Democrats appears to be that there is strength in numbers. The more names there are on a precinct voter list, the more potential votes that can be recorded on Election Day (or before, or both, as we've seen). If the name "Robert J. Voter" is on the list, *some* voter can sign the voter log in that space and cast a vote, and no one will ever question that vote.

Think of a name on a voter roll as a place holder, just waiting for a vote to be recorded. As you've read in actual accounts from Republican poll watchers, huge numbers of voters on Election Day can overwhelm poll workers and make an any real intervention against fraud nearly impossible.

We've all seen stories in recent years of the ridiculous number of fraudulent voters that are "registered" by Democrats and Democratic Party affiliated organizations. While this practice has been around for decades, it has never been practiced more often, or more blatantly, than it has in recent years by the Association of Community Organizers for Reform Now, or ACORN.

ACORN, as we outlined earlier in Nevada, is to voter fraud what Babe Ruth was to the home run - they didn't invent it but they certainly made it famous. At least 52 individuals who worked for ACORN or its affiliates have been CONVICTED of voter registration fraud. ACORN itself was convicted in that Nevada investigation in 2008 of illegal compensation, where they illegally paid voter registration canvassers cash bonuses for exceeding their quotas.

As you read about those infractions, ACORN submitted 91,002 registration forms in Clark County, of which only 23,186 – only about 1/4th - turned out to be valid new voters, according to Secretary of State Ross Miller. An indictment with 13 counts was handed down against ACORN and their Las Vegas Field Director, Christopher Edwards.

Also, in 2008, Washington state prosecutors fined ACORN $25,000 after multiple employees were found guilty of voter registration fraud. In September 2009, 11 ACORN workers were accused of forging voter registration applications in Miami-Dade County during the previous election. The Florida state attorney's office found 197 of 260 contained personal ID information that did not match any living person.

Believe me, this is just the tip of the iceberg. I could have written a book that looked like War and Peace if I'd included every single example out there on the way Democrats stuff the registration box. Take the time to do your own search on ACORN and fraudulent voter registration. Pack a lunch.

One of the very best examples of this fraudulent voter registration is Project Vote. An ACORN affiliate, they generated over 1.1 million new voter registrations across America in 2008. Incredibly, election officials *invalidated over 400,000* of those registrations filed – over 36%. It's unlikely that this can be explained away as innocent mistakes, and this is *only one* of the many groups out there generating fraudulent voter registrations. And remember:

These are just the ones they caught. How many invalid registrations made it through?

A woman named Anita Moncrief, who worked at Project Vote, came forward as a whistleblower against ACORN. Not surprising to any of us, she stated that ACORN's development director, Karen Gillette, had told her:

- That she (Ms. Gillette) had direct contact with the 2008 Obama campaign.
- That she (Ms. Moncrief) was instructed by Ms. Gillette to call Obama donors who had "maxed out" on campaign donations but who could contribute to Project Vote.

As further proof of the link between Obama and ACORN during the 2008 election, Citizen's Consulting, Inc., a group controlling ACORN, was paid $832,000 by the Obama campaign for turnout efforts in key states.

As I said, you can do your own search, and you will find literally dozens of reports of liberal and/or Democratic groups found registering fraudulent voters all across the fruited plain. Actually, mostly in urban areas, because as you saw in our earlier review of specific states, these really are the only areas Democrats can win – high population districts where they have enough population and potential to create a high number of fraudulent registrations and where they also have control.

Once these groups have gone to all the time and expense to get these "voters" registered, the next step is to ensure that all of those registered voters, legitimate or otherwise, are <u>never</u> removed from the voter rolls.

It requires considerable diligence and a concerted effort on the part of the states to continually update their voter rolls. Congress passed a law that requires them to do so in 1993 called the National Voter Registration Act, better known as the Motor Voter law. Section 8 of that law specifically mandates that the states must continually remove ineligible voters from their registration lists.

Prior to the 2012 election, True the Vote sent legal notices to 160 counties across the US asking that they do just that. They alleged that all of these 160 counties had more voters on their registration rolls than actual live, eligible voters, based on the most recent Census.

True the Vote correctly pointed out that these counties may therefore be in violation of Section 8 of the National Voter Registration Act. Again, this portion of the legislation mandates that they remove dead people, people who have moved away, or for whatever reason that are no longer eligible to vote.

The 160 counties in question are located in 19 different states that account for 203 Electoral College votes. Among these 19 states are six critical battleground states, and listed among the biggest offending counties were:

- LaSalle, Ill., with 520 percent voter registration.
- Jefferson, Miss., with more than 230 percent.
- Hanson, S.D. with 165 percent.

After True the Vote sent legal notices to these 160 counties, informing them that they had too many people registered to vote in their counties and needed to follow the law and do something about it, the response from those counties was almost non-existent in most cases. This was for a very simple reason.

They knew they didn't have to. They knew that the Obama/Holder DOJ had their back.

We'll talk about this in more detail later, but under Eric Holder, the Civil Rights Division of the US Justice Department has refused to enforce Section 8 of the National Voter Registration Act, and these counties knew it.

How big a problem is this? According to a study released in 2012 by the nonprofit Pew Center on the States, one in eight voter registrations in the United States is no longer valid or is "significantly inaccurate." An estimated *24 million* faulty voter registrations were estimated to be on the books nationwide, including 1.8 million dead people listed as active voters.

What's perhaps more frightening is that the Pew Center also discovered that some 2.8 million people have active registrations in more than one state. Remember the people from Florida, Kentucky, and Tennessee who were caught voting in Ohio? Allowing people to continue to be registered in multiple states allows for this kind of abuse. In other words, there are 2.8 million voters who could go vote both in their home state and also vote in the battleground state of their choice.

We know three of those people wound up voting in Ohio.

How many others were there?

Democrats will argue that these are rare examples, and that voter fraud hardly ever happens. Those of us who claim that we take the integrity of our ballots seriously are just trying to create fear over nothing, and our true motive is to suppress the votes of the poor and the downtrodden.

However, looking back to Ohio, the Columbus Dispatch (hardly a conservative paper) published an article prior to the election stating that "more than one out of every five registered Ohio voters is probably ineligible to vote."

The article went on to note that in two counties the number of registered voters exceeded the number of eligible voters in the county. Ohio's Wood County shows 109 registered voters for every 100 eligible. These numbers have been contested and there has been much back and forth as to how many actual eligible voters there were versus the number who registered, and then voted. Democrats also argue that this is simply the result of many students who attended Bowling Green University, and who were once registered there, having not been removed from the voter rolls.

Lawrence County, according to the Dispatch, had 104 voters registered per 100 eligible. These were by no means isolated incidents as the article went on to pointed out that there were *31 other counties with over 90 percent voter registration*, a figure that is over *20 percent higher* than the national average.

Is it just a happy coincidence, that in the single most important state in the election, voter registrations were more than 20% above the national average? Or is it possible that Ohio is simply a state where the voters are more enthusiastic and involved than the average voters?

It doesn't appear that enthusiasm is the answer, given that approximately 1.6 million of the 7.8 million registered voters in the state haven't bothered to vote in at least four years. Since a lot of these people only show up to vote every four years, we'll just have to go with happy coincidence.

Democrats tell us that these errors in voter registrations are simply a matter of vast numbers of names in thousands of counties, and that some degree of inaccuracy is to be expected. That's true, and some of these faulty registrations can be chalked up to bureaucracy and are probably the result of honest mistakes. Many fraudulent registrations, however, were put there with malicious intent, to use a legal term, and Democrats absolutely have gone to great extremes to keep as many of these names on the books as possible.

Despite the efforts of Obama and Holder, many groups and legislatures in several states are trying to clean up this mess. The American Civil Rights Union filed suit against two counties in Mississippi that have more registered voters than the Census says they have voting-eligible citizens.

Three former Justice Department lawyers filed lawsuits against Jefferson Davis County and Walthall County. The complaints outline that the US Census says Jefferson Davis County has only 9,536 residents of voting age. Yet the county has 10,078 registered voters, giving it a registration rate of 105%. Walthall County rolls are even worse, with the Census showing only 11,368 voting-age residents there, but having 14,108 registered voters, good for a 124% registration rate. For the record, the national average is about 70%.

The Indiana General Assembly has begun the process of cleaning up Indiana's voter registration rolls. They cite bloated voter rolls in every one of the state's 92 counties that contain the names of people who have moved away, are in prison or have died. Indiana Secretary of State Connie Lawson championed the funding for the project, citing the need to maintain the integrity of elections and to meet requirements of state and federal laws.

As stated earlier, the more names there are on voter rolls, the more opportunities there are to have someone, anyone, show up and record a vote. Connie Lawson summed up very nicely the reason that all states need to fix this problem, and what is at stake in all future elections:

> *"Every duplicate name and every bad address is just an opportunity for vote fraud."*

You know it, I know it, and don't kid yourself, so do the Democrats. The next step in the voter fraud playbook is to do what they try to tell us "hardly ever" happens:

> To generate actual votes for their candidates, by ensuring that *someone* shows up on Election Day (or before, or both) and

votes under the names of all of those "registered voters," legitimate or otherwise.

Certainly, millions of the votes recorded for Obama were legitimate, but it is just as certain based on the evidence that many were not. If you want to hear a description of how it's done by someone who's done it, read the following interview published in an article by American Thinker on July 6, 2012. The article, written by Lee Cary, detailed an interview he'd conducted with a member of the Chicago political machine. It contained the following:

> *"In Chicago, the Precinct Captains watch to see who votes and who doesn't. Then, at the end of the day, others will cast votes for those who haven't shown up to vote, all under the direction of the Precinct Captain. If the actual voter shows up later, they're given someone else's card. The Republican poll watchers don't stop this. Hell, most of them are actually Democrats."*

Think of what we were told by poll watchers in Ohio, Florida, and Virginia. All of them said they saw individuals come in and vote more than once, saw people allowed to vote who didn't know their address (at least not until a friendly Democratic poll watcher either told them or showed them the computer screen), saw busloads of people brought into vote, and witnessed these and other occurrences of voter fraud dozens and dozens of times.

Speaking of poll watchers, keep in mind that on election day 2012, not only did we hear some of their tales of rampant voter fraud, but remember that Republican poll watchers were forcibly expelled from polling places all over Philadelphia, many of which then went on to record 99% of the vote for Obama. In Columbus, Ohio, hundreds of Republican poll watchers weren't permitted into polling places by Democratic poll judges ostensibly due to "faulty paperwork." In Florida, a poll watcher was denied access on Election Day after reporting irregularities in early voting. Where Democrats have control of the polling places, there are a multitude of such examples of them working to avoid having any of their opponents present to monitor their actions.

Democrats continue to insist that there's no such thing as voter fraud, at least not in any significant numbers. When confronted with all of these thousands of fraudulent registrations, they're always quick to explain them away, or at least to minimize any possible harm in them, by telling us that it really isn't voter fraud until someone actually votes illegally.

Congressman Jesse Jackson, Jr. (D-Ill.) summed up the Democratic position on this, after the names of several Dallas Cowboys showed up on voter rolls in the aforementioned Nevada case in 2008, along with many other falsified registrations, when he was quoted as saying:

> *"Obviously it's not right for a fake 'Tony Romo' to be registered in Las Vegas ... but remember the basic point - it's not voter fraud unless someone shows up at the voting booth on Election Day and tries to pass himself off as 'Tony Romo.'"*

Jackson and other Democrats want desperately for Americans to believe that there is no problem. They declare that "as long as people aren't being caught voting illegally, there must not be any illegal voting going on." You see them on cable news shows all the time, talking about the *"Republican obsession with 'non-existent voter fraud.'"*

Of all the disingenuous Big Lies told by Democrats about voter fraud, this is the second most offensive.

It's a self-fulfilling prophecy for them, because they know that as long as a photo ID isn't required, and that they can control what happens in many of these voting precincts, PEOPLE WON'T GET CAUGHT. Think through this example with me:

- The name "Robert J. Voter" is on the roll.
- I show up and say I'm Robert J. Voter.
- No ID is required, and/or I'm given assistance by a friendly Democratic poll worker to help me identify myself.
- I sign the book, I vote.
- With electronic voting, there is no paper trail.

How would this illegal vote ever be caught? How would anyone ever know? No one would, and Democrats know it. They know we'll never be able to identify these false votes, and that's why they fight so hard to keep this system rolling. The point Mr. Jackson and other Democrats are deliberately misleading you about is an important one—PEOPLE ARE showing up in voting booths on election day and passing themselves off as someone else. People are voting illegally, and they're doing it by the tens of thousands.

One very important and simple step to stop one person from voting under another person's name is by demanding that the person voting can positively identify himself. To most of us, presenting a photo ID when we vote seems not only reasonable but in fact imperative. In virtually every state in the union, you need a photo ID to buy alcohol, or cigarettes, to enter an R rated movie, and you certainly need one to board an airplane.

You may even be one of the people who are astonished that anyone would be against it, and by the fact that Democrats fight tooth and nail against voter ID laws, as if they were fighting for the very air that they breathe.

You shouldn't be surprised, because simply put they're doing just that, they're fighting for their survival. The fact is that their odds of winning a presidential election without voter fraud are very slim, and a good many of them know it.

Many Democrats know that if all states required a photo ID to vote, Mitt Romney would now be President. If anyone wants to challenge that statement, consider this:

> In the 2012 presidential election, Barack Obama didn't win a single state that requires a photo ID in order to vote. Not one.

We've touched on the election results in Pennsylvania, and how the incredible margins in many precincts in Philadelphia led to an Obama victory in the state. It is important to note that none of the voters in the state of Pennsylvania were required to show a photo ID in order to cast a vote, including the thousands who voted in the Philadelphia precincts where Republican poll watchers were forcibly removed for many hours on Election Day.

Judge Robert Simpson of the Commonwealth Court of Pennsylvania had originally upheld a voter ID law in August when liberal groups challenged it, but the state's Supreme Court instructed him to hold additional hearings on whether enough had been done to make sure everyone had access to photo

IDs. On October 2, he ruled that the voter ID law be put on hold, stating that election officials could ask voters for photo identification but could not require it.

For the record, a large majority of Pennsylvania voters supported the law which would require photo identification to vote, according to a poll in September 2012 by Quinnipiac University/New York Times/CBS News (none of which are exactly conservative think tanks). Their poll found that the law was backed by 62 percent of likely voters, including about 9 of 10 Republicans and two-thirds of independents. To no one's surprise, most members of the Voter Fraud Party were opposed to the law.

Thirty states have Voter IDs laws in some form. As stated above, the intent is simply to ensure that a voter is they say they are and isn't trying to vote under someone else's name. Indiana became the first state to enact a strict photo ID law in 2006, a law that was upheld by the Supreme Court two years later.

Along with Indiana, Tennessee, Kansas and Georgia have the toughest voter ID laws. These states won't allow voters to cast a regular ballot without first showing valid photo ID. If they cannot, these voters are allowed to submit a provisional ballot, and must produce the mandatory ID within a certain time frame and affirm in person or writing they are the same individual who filled out a temporary ballot on Election Day.

Those who oppose voter ID laws say that they disproportionately affect elderly, minority and low-income groups. While these groups may indeed be less likely to have a photo ID, in a study by the Brennan Center, among voters who said they were "certain to vote" only 1 percent said they didn't have a proper ID.

This battle has been ongoing. Not surprisingly, it's drawn along party lines, and in many cases comes down to whoever has control of the courts, the state legislatures, or the Governor's office.

After Republican-led legislatures passed laws last year in Minnesota, Missouri, New Hampshire and North Carolina, their Democratic governors vetoed them. In New Hampshire, the legislature was able to override the governor's veto.

Two judges in Wisconsin blocked the enforcement of the state's photo ID law. Their state attorney general has tried unsuccessfully to have the Wisconsin Supreme Court intervene and reinstate the law prior to the November election.

Some states, including Michigan, Hawaii, Louisiana, Florida, Idaho, and South Dakota – sort of have a voter ID law. Voters are asked for a photo ID, but if they can't provide one, they're asked to sign affidavits that they are who they say they, and possibly provide a signature to compare with registration records.

Democrats know they risk looking foolish by arguing against showing an ID to vote, so they do what any good Liberal does when they know that they can't win an argument based on merit or fact (which incidentally is all the time) they change the subject and engage in personal attacks and accusations against their opponent.

This brings us to <u>the most offensive</u> Big Lie told by Democrats about voter fraud:

> If you think people need to show a photo ID in order to vote,
> or if you believe there is any such thing as voter fraud, you
> are obviously a racist.

If you want to do your own search on voter fraud and racism, you will find literally *hundreds* of Liberals and Democrats opining that every voter ID law is passed to suppress minority voting, not to combat voter fraud. If you're watching cable news, or CSPAN, and at any point come across any debate on voter ID and voter fraud, it is absolutely impossible to witness such a debate without some member of the Democratic Party or one of their supporters declare that this is out and out racism.

Attorney General Eric Holder and others have gone so far to compare voter ID requirements to poll tax laws, laws passed in the old south designed to discourage voting by blacks. We have chronicled here how his Department of Justice clearly sees such issues along racial lines, when Tom Perez, who headed up the Civil Rights division of the DOJ, told the IG that in his opinion, Section 5 of the Voting Rights Act does not protect white voters from racial discrimination.

Holder has also made extensive use of Section 5 of the Voting Rights Act. This law says that any state with a history of discrimination must receive pre-clearance before they are allowed to make any changes to voting laws. He used this to block stricter voter ID laws in both Texas and South Carolina. Thankfully, the Supreme Court finally did away with this outrageous and outdated law in June of 2013.

Democrats know there's nothing worse for any politician, and nothing that they're more frightened of, than to be tagged as a racist. At any mention of stricter voter ID laws, or of reducing voter fraud, they will label the proponents as racist in an attempt to change the argument and to derail their opponents.

As I said above, this is a common tactic by Liberals, and one they employ quite often. To be fair, Liberals really don't have much choice. In this debate, as is the case with virtually all debates between Conservatives and Liberals, Liberals are burdened by the fact that none of the facts support their argument. Knowing that they can't prevail based on the facts, they really only have three alternatives:

- Acknowledge that their argument is false and do what is right.
- Make up facts as they go along.
- Change the subject and tell lies about their opponent.

As we're all painfully aware, Liberals will choose the second and third options just about every time. This debate, given the paramount importance it has to their very survival, will certainly not be an exception. Democrats will fight to the death against any attempt to reduce voter fraud, because they know that reducing voter fraud could indeed be the death of their party.

How well has this playbook worked for Democrats? While the following is by no means a complete list, it does provide just a few of their crowning achievements in voter fraud both in this election and in recent years:

- The "Miracle of Vice" reelection of Harry Reid, where he overcame a four-point deficit and turned it into a six-point victory in one week, amid allegations that voting machines already were programmed to vote for Reid. The SEIU has the exclusive contract to service electronic voting machines in Clark County, Nevada, where about one half the state's votes are cast.
- The defeat of Allen West in 2012, by less than 2500 votes, when 4000 votes were possibly switched amid other allegations of irregularities, yet there was never a full investigation or recount.
- Twelve thousand noncitizens registered to vote in Colorado, with 5,000 of them apparently voting in 2010.

- Al Franken being elected on the illegally-cast votes of incarcerated convicts. Millions had voted in the Minnesota election, but the votes of 341 criminals disenfranchised an entire state. The Secretary of State in Minnesota who oversaw this, incidentally, was a man who was elected with huge financial support from non-other than George Soros.

- In Tennessee, District 4 Election Commissioner Carl Payne reported a number of incidents in his own November race. In one, a father cast an absentee ballot, the son voted in person and then the son changed clothes and then returned to vote as his father, based on a written statement from the poll manager. Another involved a voter who came to cast a ballot, gave a name that was on the poll book, signed the receipt book and was allowed to vote. Another person using the same name came to vote later that day, and was informed he'd already voted. Finally, a voter cast a ballot in person at the proper precinct, then left and turned in a provisional ballot, including a sworn affidavit, at another precinct."

- In another example of multiple voting, a man named Mike Hays was alleged according to court documents to be registered to vote in both Mohave County and Coconino County, Arizona. Hays used a campaign worker's address in Kingman, in Mohave County, but actually lived in Flagstaff, in Coconino County. Hays was also running for Sheriff of Mohave County, and apparently filed the same false address when he ran for Sheriff.

- The case in Troy, New York, where Democrats were accused of falsifying absentee ballots. A total of four Democratic officials and political operatives plead guilty to voter fraud-related felony charges in an alleged scheme to steal a New York election.

- The case in Missouri where numerous counties had more ballots cast in the 2004 elections than there were eligible voters. This case went to trial, and would have been won, but it was dropped by the Obama Department of Justice shortly after he took office.

- Two brothers, William and Braulio Manzano of Mower County in Minnesota, two non-citizens, were charged with illegally signing the portion of their voting application that indicated they were citizens who could vote. Also, in Minnesota, a man from Cottage Grove told police that on Election Day someone had committed voter fraud by signing under his name at his polling place, thus making it impossible for him to vote.

- The Obama/Holder DOJ also dropped the case involving Black Panthers standing outside a polling place with batons. Afterward, a "whistleblower" by the name of J. Christian Adams testified on the Department of Justice's unwillingness to pursue voter related crimes committed by people of color.

- In the 1996 Congressional election between Bob Dornan and Loretta Sanchez, Dornan led Sanchez by 233 votes the day after the election, but one week and 12,000 absentee ballots later Sanchez had a 929-vote margin. Dornan specifically charged that a Latino rights group and the Democratic Party signed up illegal voters in a drive he said led to "the first case in history where a congressional election was decided by non-citizens."

- In Bucks County, Pennsylvania a Democrat candidate flooded the voter registration office with fraudulent applications for absentee ballots.

- Voting machines in North Carolina and Nevada which are "voting" for Democrats even when that is the exact opposite of what voters intend. Of all kinds of other fraud going on, this is the worst—actual changing of votes.

- Democrats in Pennsylvania created a fictitious "Pennsylvania Voter Assistance Office" to commit voter fraud.

- A woman who is literally under criminal indictment for past voter fraud with liberal A.C.O.R.N. now heading up yet another corrupt liberal voter fraud group.

- In 2011 there were investigations, indictments or convictions for voter fraud in California, Texas, Minnesota, Indiana, Ohio, Georgia, North Carolina and Maryland. In all but one case, those alleged to have committed fraud were Democrats.

- According to an article in the Boston Globe in January 2013, the US attorney's office charged Stephen "Stat" Smith, a member of the Massachusetts legislature, with allegedly submitting fraudulent requests for absentee ballots, then knowingly casting those ballots on behalf of voters without their knowledge. They also alleged that Smith delivered absentee ballots to ineligible voters so that they could cast said ballots in his favor. Smith faces up to two years in prison, and was also required to vacate his seat in the Legislature.

The Democratic Party has become, for all intents and purposes, the Voter Fraud Party. They've relied on it for decades, but have escalated these efforts in recent years, beginning in earnest with the 2000 elections and in each election since. There is simply too much evidence of wrongdoing, in too many states by too many people, to conclude otherwise.

As much as this threatens the outcome and integrity of all future elections, these efforts at voter fraud pale in comparison to the Obama teams' latest strategies, which we will detail in the following pages. If left unchecked, these new tactics, combined with their rampant voter fraud, could very well mean that we've seen the last legitimate election perhaps ever in the USA.

Obama's New Democratic Playbook for the 21st Century

While Democrats certainly have much to be proud of (or ashamed of, depending on your point of view) with regard to their effectiveness in fraudulently changing elections, the Obama White House has embarked on an even more aggressive, even more terrifying, and even more unconstitutional set of strategies.

As despicable and un-American as the old voter fraud playbook is, these new tactics the Obama administration is employing are far more insidious and in the long run far more destructive. They involve an administration utilizing the full force of the federal government not to do the work of the people as mandated by our Constitution, but instead using that power as a political tool.

While not all of these tactics are completely new, they all have been enhanced, and in some cases, brought to unprecedented heights under this White House and its reelection team. As a reminder, these newest strategies are:

1. Buy votes, by promising to give as much money as possible to as many people as possible for as many things as possible.
2. Bring in donations from anywhere and everywhere, legal or otherwise.
3. Utilize the full force and intimidation of the United States government, primarily the IRS, to harass and suppress the efforts of their political opponents.

4. Use the new technology available, such as electronic voting machines, to their advantage whenever possible.

5. Ensure that everyone who was willing to conduct any of the above activities on their behalf knew that they could do so with impunity, and that they could carry out these activities without fear of prosecution.

The following pages will outline how, by following their voter fraud playbook and by employing these tactics, Obama and the Democrats were able to steal the 2012 election.

WOULD YOU HAVE VOTED FOR OBAMA FOR $32,000?

Throughout the 2012 campaign I repeatedly told people that if I were offered $1,000,000 in cash I would not have voted for Barack Obama. Though some people challenged me on it, I absolutely meant it and would not have cast my ballot for Barack for any amount of money.

Why do I ask if you'd have voted for him for $32,000? It's because a lot of people did vote for him for that very amount, on average. There are now 67 million Americans getting a check in some form from the federal government, and $32,000 is the average amount of our tax dollars that these 67 million people are receiving per year. That's 2.2 trillion dollars a year for those of you keeping score.

Since the day he took office, Barack Obama has been on a mission to increase the number of Americans getting money from our government, and he has been immensely successful at doing so. In fact, that 67-million-person number is up 23% since Obama was inaugurated, and there's nothing accidental about that.

One of the central strategies of the Obama presidency, and of his reelection campaign, was to appeal to the masses by promising them that he would take money from other (less deserving) Americans and give it to them. Obama's spin on of John F. Kennedy's famous plea to Americans during his inauguration speech was something like this:

> *Ask not what you can do for your country, Ask instead what your country can do for you.*

The strategy is really very simple. The more people you can make dependent on your policies and big government, the more people who will have no choice but to vote for your policies and big government. Obama's goal was to create millions of voters who, simply put, couldn't afford NOT to vote for him. If you put people on the gravy train, they'll vote to elect the guy who keeps the gravy train running.

While the purchase of votes may sound like old Democratic Party news to some of you, I don't believe any campaign in history has engaged in the practice to anywhere near to the degree the Obama campaign did.

Let's start with food stamps. When Obama was inaugurated in January 2009, the number of SNAP recipients was about 32 million. By October 2012 that number had jumped to 48 million. For those of you who aren't good with numbers *that's a 50% increase in four years.*

It also means that the food stamp program added approximately 11,133 recipients *per day* from January 2009 to October 2012. This massive increase led Republican candidate Newt Gingrich to refer to Obama as "the food stamp President." While this caused much indignation on the part of Democrats, given the numbers it's tough to argue with.

In an effort to help achieve these high numbers, Obama had his Department of Agriculture run radio ads for months leading up to the election. Spending reached $41 million dollars in 2011, roughly a 530% increase over the $6.5 million spent as recently as the year 2000. I'm not sure if the 2011 figure includes the spending on advertising for the food stamp program in Mexico.

Yes, Mexico. Our government is running ads in Mexico to promote the SNAP program. In May 2013, there was an amendment sponsored by Senate Republican Jeff Sessions of Alabama to cut off advertising for the food stamp program on foreign soil. The amendment never made it out of committee, with Democrats holding the partly line to kill it.

Why would elected officials be so invested in actually getting more people enrolled in this program? Ask yourself a question. If you were a food stamp recipient, and Obama is continually talking about making them more available, not less, how would that affect your vote? Obama sees this as 16,000,000 more people who need his government, therefore millions more in potential voters.

Another example of Barack Obama's success in getting more Americans dependent on government is the massive increase in the number of Americans now collecting disability. The number of Americans leaving the workforce under Obama to permanently claim disability benefits is unlike anything ever before seen. I offer the following sickening statistic:

In March of 2013, the number of people who signed up with the federal government's permanent worker disability program was virtually the same as the number of people who got jobs.

During that month, 81,804 workers left the workforce to join the Social Security Disability Insurance program, or SSDI. That number wasn't unusually high, as in the first 3 months of 2013 nearly a quarter million workers joined the program, which is pretty much on pace with where it's been ever since Barack Obama took office.

During the first Obama term, *4 million people* left the workforce to go on disability. As of April 1, 2013, the ranks of the disabled number 8.8 million, and when you add in children and spouses the number climbs to 10.9 million, an increase of over 20%.

Why would disabilities increase by 20% percent under the Obama administration? Typically, disabilities rise as does the population, which has increased only about 4%.

The answer appears to be twofold. The anemic economic recovery under Obama has created far fewer jobs and hence far more need. Perhaps even more significantly, the Social Security administration has made receiving disability benefits *much easier and much more expedient*. The Social Security Administration under Obama:

- Places more weight on self-reported pain and discomfort. Perhaps as a result, the share of disability as a result of back pain rose from 13% in 1983 to 28% in 2010.
- Has relaxed the screening of mental illness. The share of disability awards for mental illness rose from 16% in 1983 to 33% in 2010

Together the above two conditions, back pain and mental illness, now account for more than half of all disabilities. Plus, of the 2.7 million workers on disability for mental disorders, a full 1.7 million, 63%, have "intellectual and mood disorders." Adding to that figure undoubtedly is the fact that people can be declared disabled if they get nervous at work, or at school, if they have attention deficit disorders, or are not very intelligent.

That last qualifier, "not very intelligent," really scares me, as it makes all liberals eligible.

Applications to receive disability benefits have also been streamlined, making them not only easier to get but also taking less time to do so. The application process can get started on-line, and applicants can receive a free call from a lawyer. To no one's surprise, law firms have inserted themselves into the process, firms that specialize in helping people with the bureaucracy and paperwork. They can even help with an appeal if the request for benefits is denied, which apparently is happening less and less.

A standard concern with people signing up for disability is that almost none ever return to the workforce, but for Barack Obama, this isn't a concern—it's a blessing. I believe that in Obama's view of America, these four million Americans who left the work force to go on disability during his term provide him with a "win/win":

1. It has created four million more voters who need the government's help and therefore can be counted to vote for him and big government.
2. It means that four million more people are no longer counted in the work force, therefore they are not counted in the unemployment numbers, helping to artificially reduce the unemployment rate.

Again, I encourage you to do a search on "Obama and disability." You will find an incredible amount of links and information to help someone find out how they too can receive SSDI benefits.

You've undoubtedly seen the "Obama Phone" video, and have seen and heard other examples of people who talked about how they no longer need to worry about their mortgage payment, or car payment, thanks to Obama. Obama spent months on the campaign trail throwing money at anyone and everyone who might be able to cast a vote. Whether it was more student loans for students, more money for illegal immigrants, more weeks of unemployment, more free contraceptives for women, more food stamps and housing, there was not a core demographic group that wasn't promised that Santa Claus was coming on November 6 this year.

All of these, however, pale by comparison. Their crowning achievement in creating dependents and voters was and is ObamaCare.

You saw how they sold ObamaCare to the American people as a means to provide health care to those who didn't have it. In truth, the primary driver behind

ObamaCare was the desire to create a whole new class of dependents, millions upon millions of Americans who would come to rely on the government to provide their healthcare. The bill was specifically designed to drive American citizens out of their employer provided plans and into the government sponsored exchanges.

Democrats went to such lengths to pass ObamaCare, even knowing they would suffer heavy losses in the 2010 mid-term elections, because they knew that if ObamaCare became law it would be the mother of all entitlement programs, and would help them achieve their goal of driving us down the path to entitlements and government dependence.

The Democratic Party strategy of creating more voters who need them and must vote for them is summed up very nicely in the following cartoon:

This cartoon perfectly captures this very important and very destructive portion of the Democratic Party strategy.

When I was growing up the Democratic Party was known as the party of the "working people." In recent years, they've really become more the party of the "non-working people." They've championed government handouts by the billions, not out of compassion as they try to claim, but as a way to pander to the poor and secure their votes. Walter Williams, the famed economist, has gone so far as to refer to the Black Congressional Caucus as the "clan with a tan," decrying their practice of providing Welfare and other aid to buy (and enslave, if you will) the votes of African Americans.

As I said earlier, Democrats have done this for years, but this last election provided a very significant difference from elections past. Historically, come election time, Democratic candidates have magically transformed themselves into fiscal conservatives. Between campaigns they spent like drunken sailors, but once campaign season rolled around, they did everything they could to convince voters that they were averse to big spending and big government. They knew they had to, or would face certain defeat.

Walter Mondale was openly liberal, as was Michael Dukakis. Both were beaten soundly in 1984 and 1988, and ever since then Liberals have run away from that word and from that ideology as if it were the plague. When it came to national elections, they knew they had to somehow convince voters that they would be prudent stewards of their tax dollars.

In 1992, Bill Clinton campaigned as a centrist, and defeated George Bush primarily by focusing on the economy. Then, in his first two years in office, Clinton veered hard left. Massive tax increases, gays in the military, and worst of all nationalized health care (HillaryCare).

What happened? The economy tanked, his approval tanked, and he faced the almost certain fate of being a one term president. Now, Bill Clinton is certainly a devoted Liberal, but the one thing Bill Clinton loved more than Liberalism was Bill Clinton, and rather than face being booted from office he hired Dick Morris to help him somehow salvage his presidency.

Morris's advice was simple—become a conservative. Morris told Clinton to sign off on Newt Gingrich's agenda in the 1994 Contract with America—cut spending, cut capital gains taxes, reduce the size of government, reform welfare. Morris advised Clinton, correctly, that these actions would result in an economic rebound, which he could then take credit for and win reelection.

And it worked, with Clinton holding onto the White House in 1996 and presiding over (Monica aside) a relatively prosperous eight-year term. If you every want to make a Liberal's head explode, simply inform them of the fact that the reason for the success of the Clinton presidency is that he became a conservative.

The point I'm making here is that throughout the recent history of American politics, candidates for President knew that in order to win they had to run as a conservative, at least with regard to fiscal issues. They knew that to openly campaign as a liberal or a "give away" candidate was electoral suicide. Even Obama, in 2008, masqueraded as a centrist figure.

That all changed in 2012. Barack Obama openly campaigned as a liberal, if not as an out and out socialist, and turned what had previously been conventional wisdom on its ear. Instead of saying "you can afford to vote for me, I won't spend your money," Obama said:

> *"You can't afford NOT to vote for me, because I will give you money."*

For the first time in my memory, a presidential candidate campaigned on a platform that was not just "tax and spend" but was really more "tax and give," as in *"I'll tax them and give it to you."* And he did it all with a giant lie, a lie he called "fairness."

Obama made his mantra of "fairness" the centerpiece of his reelection. He told us that all Americans need to pay their "fair share," and that the richest 1% weren't doing that. He told us that the only way to pay down the debt, and for us to be able to pay our bills, was for all Americans to pay their fair share. If everyone did that, our fiscal house would be in order.

These are what we refer to as "lies," for two very important reasons:

- First of all, the wealthiest 1% of the population pays approximately 37% of the total tax burden. It what universe is 1% of the population paying 37% of the tax bill not fair?
- Secondly, his claims that the increases he wanted to make in the marginal tax rates to achieve "fairness" would balance the budget and pay down the debt were mathematically preposterous.

To illustrate just how disingenuous this was, let's pretend that Obama was right in saying that these greedy, no good wealthy people need to be taxed more. In fact, let's pass a law that:

In 2014, the wealthiest 1% of Americans must pay a _100%_ income tax

For the purpose of this exercise, we're going to need to "pretend" that several things are true no matter how ridiculous they are, such as:

- That this wouldn't make us Communist China. (It would)
- That taking all of this money out of the US economy wouldn't dramatically reduce other revenues, and that these would be new, incremental dollars. (They wouldn't be)
- That taking all of this income from people who spend a lot wouldn't be devastating to the economy and wouldn't drive unemployment even higher. (It would)
- That the US Congress would then apply every single penny of this new incremental revenue directly to the deficit. (They wouldn't)

Now, even if all of the above were true (*which none of it is*), what happens?

- YOU WOULD RAISE ABOUT **1.2 TRILLION DOLLARS** TO PAY ON THE DEBT.
- WE WOULD STILL OWE OVER 15 TRILLION DOLLARS.
- CONGRATULATIONS. YOU JUST DESTROYED OUR ECONOMY TO PAY OFF ABOUT 6% OF OUR DEBT.

This clearly illustrates what a ridiculously lie Obama was telling. Even if you raised the taxes of the top 1% *to a rate of 100% for a year, it wouldn't make much of a difference.* How on earth could you argue that a few percentages would help?

But as is typically the case, Liberals were not going to let a little thing like the truth get in the way of a really good campaign strategy. They continued to pound away at this "fairness" message, and sadly it appears to have worked. Polls taken throughout the campaign clearly showed that a significant portion of the electorate was buying into it, and exit polling on Election Day seemed to confirm it.

When voters were asked on Nov. 6 whether they favored raising taxes to reduce the deficit, a total of 60 percent said "yes." A full 47 percent favored increasing taxes for those who earn $250,000 or more, and 13 percent actually approved of tax increases for all.

This is of course the exact opposite of what needs to be done.

We don't have an "under taxing" problem, we have an "over-spending" problem. The exercise above illustrates that we cannot possibly tax the wealthy enough to both sustain current spending levels and cut our debt.

Happily, there is a solution, one which has been proven time and time again. WE NEED TO CUT TAXES. Four times in the past 100 years our government has reduced marginal tax rates, and each time we did two things happened:

- The economy took off, and generated some of the greatest economic booms in our history.
- Revenues to the treasury increased due to the corresponding economic growth.

After Reagan's tax cuts in 1981, in which the highest marginal rates were dramatically reduced, revenues to the federal treasury skyrocketed due to the resulting economic boom. From 1982 to 1992, revenues went from about $600 billion per year to over $1.1 trillion, or nearly doubled.

Obama and his minions have repeatedly said that they took over a real mess, and that given more time their plans of more taxation, more spending, more government, and more regulation will work. In truth, it has never worked, and in fact all we need do is look at Europe, and at the countries that have followed Obama's formula all the way into collapse and bankruptcy.

Ronald Reagan took over a far worse economy in 1981, and by the end of his first term our economy was booming. By the fourth year of his first term, the economy was growing at about a 7% annual rate. Why? Because Reagan understood that the path to recovery is the very same path that made our country great in the first place – individual liberty, individual responsibility, free enterprise, less taxation, and less government.

Obama has followed just the opposite path, with more government, more taxation, less freedom, less personal responsibility, and less personal liberty. If you do the exact opposite of what made America great, you get the opposite of great. You get the abysmal results we now have.

Many people have understood for decades the true genius of this incredible experiment and unique creation called America. In the 1800s, the French sent Alexis de Tocqueville to the USA to study our democracy. He wrote a book in 1835 entitled *On Democracy in America*, and in it he was famously quoted as saying:

"The American Republic will endure until the day Congress discovers that it can bribe the public with the public's money."

Obama not only understood this, he was counting on it. His reelection in 2012 clearly showed how prophetic de Tocqueville was. Obama realized that many voters could be bribed by promising them other people's money, and in fact he centered his entire reelection campaign around that very strategy.

What's frightening is that it appears that for the first time in our history, America has reached a point where this kind of campaign can work. There are apparently far too many people who don't understand that what made America the greatest nation in the history of the world was self-reliance, individual liberty, and the promise of equality of opportunity for all Americans.

For the first time in our history, a presidential election was won by a candidate who campaigned *against* these things, and who sold Americans on the concept that the government can take care of you better than you can take care of yourself. De Tocqueville put it far better than I can:

"Democracy extends the sphere of individual freedom, socialism restricts it. Democracy attaches all possible value to each man; socialism makes each man a mere agent, a mere number. Democracy and socialism have nothing in common but one word: equality. But notice the difference: while democracy seeks equality in liberty, socialism seeks equality in restraint and servitude."

De Tocqueville's contrast between American Democracy and Socialism is striking, and absolutely dead on. It seems ironic to me that de Tocqueville and the French were striving to understand how Europe could be more like America. Obama is conversely trying to make America more like Europe. If you believe in what made America great, versus what Obama is advocating, how much further down this path do you think America can afford to go?

In Through the Lines Come a Bundle of Cash

Remember the line from the theme song from the Beverly Hillbillies, *"up through the ground come a bubblin' crude"*? For Barack Obama and his campaign, the line more accurately would be "in through the lines come a bundle of cash." Internet lines, that is. The Obama campaigns were widely renowned for their ability to raise money on-line, and below you will read just how much money they pulled in on line, and just how suspicious much of that pile of cash was.

One cardinal rule of fundraising is to widen your base of contributors, to increase the pool of those who become donors. If you could, for example, expand your potential pool of contributors from just over 300 million people to over 7 billion people, it would stand to reason that you could raise more money. If you happened to be running for President, and you were somehow able to expand your potential contributors from "citizens of the United States" to "citizens of the world," that would be the net effect. A potential drawback to this for a presidential candidate, of course, is that it happens to be against the law.

During a speech he gave in Berlin in 2008, presidential candidate Barack Obama told his audience that he was speaking to them not as a candidate for president of the United States, but as a "fellow citizen of the world." Little did we know that this was really his way of signaling his approach to campaign financing. It now appears that he was telling them that since we are, after all, all "citizens of the world," all of them could contribute to his campaigns.

According to a report by the GAI (Government Accountability Institute), many citizens of the world have done just that, providing his campaign with millions in contributions. The report contained the following warning:

> *"With millions of online campaign donations ricocheting through cyberspace, one might think the FCC would have erected serious walls to guard federal elections from foreign or fraudulent Internet contributions. But that's far from true. In fact, campaigns are largely expected to police these matters themselves."*

In other words, there is virtually no oversight into the millions of internet donations that pour into political campaigns. The report went on to note that this was especially concerning with the Obama campaign, because one of their internet sites, Obama.com, wasn't even owned by the Obama campaign. According to their report, Obama.com is owned by a China based American businessman by the name of Robert Roche. Mr. Roche is the CEO of Acorn International, a large media company. There have also been reports that Mr. Roche, an Obama bundler, has questionable business ties to state-run Chinese enterprises. I'm not really sure if the "Acorn" thing is a coincidence or not, but according to the authors of the report: 68 percent of the 2,000 visitors each day on Obama.com were foreign in origin.

What would stop non-citizens from making contributions? The answer is nothing, as long as they're small in size, or can be made to look that way, as you're going to see.

GAI has investigated the influence of foreign online campaign donations not only for Obama, but in House and Senate elections as well. Their investigations were conducted with the guidance of a former US attorney, and reportedly utilized what is known as "spidering" software, which found literally thousands of foreign sites linking to various campaign donation pages.

Dick Morris, the former Clinton campaign advisor and now staunch Obama critic, has written and spoken extensively about the problems with Obama's fundraising efforts. In a column you can find on his website, he made this chilling observation:

"In September, the Obama campaign got 1.8 million donations from small contributors who did not break the $200 threshold requiring that their information be reported to the Federal Elections Commission. They gave the campaign 98 percent of the $181 million it raised that month, a figure vastly higher than its take in any previous month."

Said another way, **only 2%** of Obama's massive amount of campaign contributions ($181M) in September 2012, *far more than they received in any other month*, had donor information reported to the FEC.

Also, according to the Obama campaign at the time, of the 1.8 million donors who contributed during the month, *over 500,000 of these were brand-new donors*, who did not contribute to the campaign either in 2008 or in 2012.

Question: Where exactly did these people supposedly come from? Are we actually supposed to believe that a half million people all suddenly came to the conclusion in September of 2012 that they really needed to contribute for the first time to the Obama campaign?

Not insignificantly, this came at a time that the Obama campaign was being dramatically outraised by the Romney campaign, and amid reports that Obama was literally running out of money.

Mitt Romney had raised $106 million in June compared to Obama's $71 million. In May, Romney, along with the Republican National Committee raised $76.8 million compared to the $60 million taken in by Obama and the Democratic National Committee. After being outraised by 28% and $17 million in May, Obama fell even further behind in June, being outraised by 49% and by $35million. ALSO, in the 18 hours after Obamacare was upheld, 47,000 people gave $4.6 million dollars to Romney's campaign.

Romney and his allies were spending nearly twice as much on television ads. All told, the Republican groups were spending $19.1 million per week in advertisements in nine battleground states, while the Obama campaign and others were spending $10.7 million per week. Republicans were spending more than Democrats per week in Colorado, Florida, Iowa, Nevada, New

Hampshire, North Carolina, Ohio, and Virginia. Obama's campaign was only outspending Republicans in one state, Pennsylvania.

The Obama campaign's fixed expenses were also extremely high. With 700 employees, the campaign was spending around $3 million a month in staff alone. In fact, at earlier points during the campaign, nearly half of Obama's spending was directed towards administrative expenses—a reflection of a campaign infrastructure that was shaped during a period *when they were anticipating raising more than $1 billion for the race.*

But donor support for Obama had absolutely fallen off a cliff compared to 2008. According to the Weekly Standard, 88 percent of the people who gave $200 or more to Obama in 2008—537,806 people—had not yet contributed that amount as of July of 2012. Donations were reflecting the fact that Obama's support had fallen off with literally every single demographic group of voters in the country.

When suddenly, almost magically, in comes $181 million dollars in September, 98% of which we have no idea as to its origin, including donations from 500,000 new donors who have suddenly decided to join the fray at this most critical moment. Which we're supposed to believe, even though we just showed you that 500,000 previous donors had bowed out.

Perhaps it was the "citizens of the world" who helped save the day. Lending credence to that theory is that the Obama campaign decided to employ a very important tool, or more accurately they decided NOT to employ this tool in their fundraising efforts. As Dick Morris went on to explain:

> *"Questions arise because the Obama campaign, unlike Romney's or, for that matter, Hillary Clinton's in 2008, refuses to ask donors for their CVV number (the number on your credit card that one is often asked for after giving one's name and expiration date). The CVV is designed to assure that the donor is actually physically holding the card."*

For the record, a CVV number (also known as CSC, CVV2 or CVN), is the three-digit securing code typically found on the back of credit cards. As Morris alludes to above, this code is used to ensure that a person making a purchase (or in this case donating money) physically possesses the card. Apparently, this lack of a CVV code requirement opens the door for all manner of shenanigans. Most specifically, it allows for accepting what are known as "robo-donations." These are large numbers of small and automatic donations made online, all of which are small enough to fall below FEC reporting requirements.

The bottom line is that we have absolutely no idea who made these donations. Well, in some cases we do. Breitbart.com reported on screen shots from Obama.com, including an email from a Canadian woman who admitted to making illegal donations:

> *"I had donated to the original campaign and will again. I would also give my vote, but alas I am a Canadian but am a staunch supporter of the Obama-Biden Team."*

After all, she's just another citizen of the world.

Whatever their motive, it is factual to say that the Obama campaign DID NOT require a CVV on their campaign donation page. For the record, 90 percent of e-commerce and 19 of the 20 largest charities in the United States use a CVV code, and it is fair to say that its use is considered standard practice in an effort to prevent fraud.

The only reason I can comprehend NOT TO require a CVV is that preventing illegal contributions is NOT your intention. I feel confident in that assertion especially when you consider the fact that the Obama campaign reportedly had to pay millions in additional fees in order to accept unsecured contributions on their donation page without the CVV code.

Think about it. If indeed the Obama campaign was truly determined to prevent illicit contributions, why would they not have employed what is considered the most basic fraud prevention tool? I'm not an expert in these matters, but I've read that these are quite easily installed, are fully automated, and do not require a great deal of continued maintenance. Ask yourself this question:

> Why would any campaign decide to pay card issuers much higher fees to receive less information about their contributors and to get less security in return, especially when doing so would reduce their ability to comply with election law?

The only logical conclusion is that the Obama campaign knew that they had much more to gain than they had to lose, and that they actually *wanted to know less about their donors*, possibly due to the fact that it allowed them to raise far more money from "citizens of the world" than they would ever lose in added fees.

The Obama campaigns loved to tout the fact that the majority of their contributions were small in nature. They told us that this was because their donations came from everyday folks, a true "grassroots" success story. Based on what we've learned, maybe there was another explanation.

Maybe, just maybe, the Obama campaigns wanted most of their donations to be under $200 so that they wouldn't have to report the name of the person making the donation to the FEC. Take a look at the following e-mail that went out from Barack Obama to thousands of his supporters:

Anthony –

In a few days, I'll be hitting the trail for my last campaign.

Everything we've accomplished in the past three years — and our chance to do so much more — is on the line.

What we do today will be a measure of whether or not we're ready to fight for it.

Donate $190 or whatever you can before tonight's fundraising deadline.

By pitching in before midnight, you'll automatically be in the running to join me and George Clooney at his place on May 10th. It's not often I can get away from work, so I look forward to spending a fun evening in L.A. with a couple supporters like you.

In the meantime, let's close out this deadline strong:

https://donate.barackobama.com/Midnight-Deadline

Thanks.

Barack

Do you think it's possible that they happen to be soliciting donations of just under $200 for a reason? Why not ask for $300, or $500?

How much of Obama's total contributions came from these donations of under $200? In both 2008 and in 2012, his campaign raised over $300 million dollars in these smaller donations. Of Obama's $500 million raised online in 2008, nearly two thirds allegedly came from these donations of under $200.

Conversely, the Romney campaign was able to raise just over $60 million in these sub-$200 contributions in 2012. I'm sure Democrats would be quick to tell us that this is because only rich fat cats voted for Romney, but perhaps it had something to do with the fact that the Romney's campaign required CVV numbers for online donations and had all standard security measures in place. To my knowledge, there are no allegations that the Romney campaign raked in millions from "citizens of the world."

Perhaps most damning of all, there is evidence that not only did the Obama campaign possibly receive millions in donations from overseas, *they aggressively and continually solicited such donations*. Referring again to the GAI report referenced above, they point to a number of foreign bloggers and other social media that outline and describe this unlawful solicitation by the Obama campaign.

- A Chinese blogger posted letters received from the Obama campaign, asking for small ($5 or less) donations.
- A member of the Italian Radical Socialist movement reported that they'd been receiving solicitations from the Obama campaign for three years.
- An Egyptian member of the board of the Union of Arab Bloggers posted solicitation letters he reported also to have received regularly receive from the Obama campaign.
- An Azerbaijani citizen received numerous solicitation letters from the Obama campaign and reposted the letters along with the numerous hyperlinks that went directly to the campaign's donation page.

One of these that contained the most specific information was from a Vietnam blogger, who writes on a website for the Vietnam Institute for Development Studies. He posted emails he'd received from the website my.barackobama.com that contained more than 24 total links to the campaign's donation page. One of these letters asking for donations that were posted on this Vietnamese domain was from Mitch Stewart, Director of the Obama campaign's "Organizing for America."

Some of these bloggers took advantage of the opportunity to contribute, some did not:

- One Norwegian blogger posted a solicitation from the Obama campaign, which included a link to their campaign donation page. When someone responded to him that non-US citizens couldn't contribute because of US elections law, he replied, "*I have in practice given money to Obama, I had done it.*"
- A Dutch blogger posted that he also received a donation request from the Obama campaign, but decided not to violate US law and contribute. He did, however, take the time to point out on his blog, "*I imagine many non-Americans have money transferred to the Obama campaign. It's just too easy.*"

The Obama campaign constantly cited these donations of under $200 as evidence that theirs was a campaign of the people. A more apt description may be that theirs was a campaign of the anonymous donor, and for a reason. The truth may well be that many of their donations, and virtually all of them in September, were reported as under $200 because those donations came from illegal sources.

While the following is not illegal, I couldn't resist including it among these other shameful Obama fundraising tactics. Appearing last summer on the Obama 2012 website, Barack Obama's campaign was officially asking people to forgo wedding or birthday gifts and donate to his campaign instead.

A post on the Obama/Biden 2012 website rolled out the "*Obama Event Registry,*" asked supporters with an upcoming birthday, wedding, or anniversary to "*support the President on your big day*" by asking for donation money in lieu of a gift." The website featured the following:

> "*Got a birthday, anniversary, or wedding coming up? Let your friends know how important this election is to you—register with Obama 2012, and ask for a donation in lieu of a gift. It's a great way to support the President on your big day. Plus, it's a gift that we can all appreciate—and goes a lot further than a gravy bowl.*"

It went on to say:

> *"Got a special milestone or event coming up? Instead of another gift card you'll forget to use, ask your friends and family for something that will go a little further: a donation for Obama for America."*

And they even provided suggested language to use when soliciting campaign cash.

> *"For my big day, I'd like to show my support for a cause I believe in—reelecting President Obama. That's why I'm asking my friends and family to donate to the Obama campaign. Thanks for chipping in!"*

Warms your heart doesn't it?

In his 2010 State of the Union Address, President Obama said: "I don't think American elections should be bankrolled by America's most powerful interests, and worse, by foreign entities."

Hypocritical, or at the very least ironic, since it certainly looks like donations from overseas, and certainly from powerful special interests such as labor unions, were instrumental in helping him win in 2012. And at a critical juncture in the campaign when his campaign was being dramatically outraised and was in danger of running out of cash, his campaign had by far its best fundraising month yet, 98% of which came from sources that will never be known. And much of that supposedly from new contributors even though old contributors were walking away in droves.

That's how Obama was able to raise enough money to "win" in 2012.

The IRS—aka the "Investigate Republicans Service"

As we now know, in the months leading up to the 2012 election the IRS was hard at work doing everything they could to limit the effectiveness of Tea Party groups. Whether this was intentional or not, and who ordered it, is still being discussed, but in 2013 the IRS admitted that it had targeted political groups applying for tax-exempt status for closer scrutiny based solely on their names or political themes. They have also admitted that the political groups they targeted were overwhelmingly conservative in nature, mostly based on having certain terms in their name—"Tea Party," "Patriot," or "9/12" most specifically.

In the 2010 mid-term elections, Tea Party groups were extremely effective, leading the way to a Republican landslide. Focusing on smaller government, less taxes, and eliminating Obamacare, Tea Party groups helped take back the House with a net gain of 63 seats and erased the gains made by Democrats in 2006 and 2008. Republicans also took control of 29 of the 50 state governorships, and gained 690 seats in state legislatures to hold their greatest number since 1928.

Barack Obama and his political team were acutely aware of this, and also had to understand that if the Tea Party groups were allowed to continue their surge, and to increase their influence in the 2012 elections, that Obama's reelection would be in grave danger. To Barack Obama's great good fortune, and perhaps based on a nudge from Obama himself or others on his team, the IRS decided to come to the rescue.

The IRS decided to stop Tea Party groups from effectively impacting the election in the simplest of ways—they stopped them from raising money. They achieved this by refusing to provide these groups with the tax-exempt status that allows them to be able to do so.

To explain how this all works, federal tax law, specifically Section 501 (c)(4), exempts certain types of nonprofit organizations from having to pay federal income tax. The language pertaining to 501(c)(4) organizations requires that such organizations be "operated exclusively for the promotion of social welfare." However, the standard that applies is that an organization "is operated *primarily* for the purpose of bringing about civic betterments and social improvements." As such, the IRS has permitted organizations described in IRC 501(c)(4) to engage in lobbying and political activities so long as those activities were not the organization's primary function.

Another benefit to having exempt status under Section 501(c)(4) as a nonprofit organization, is that they are not required to reveal the names of their donors or the amounts individual donors have contributed. Nonprofit organizations aren't required to apply for IRS certification in order to operate under Section 501(c)(4) tax exemption rules, but being certified by the IRS helps such organizations attract more donations. As I said above, this provided the linchpin for the IRS plan—stop these Tea Party groups from achieving certification, reduce the money they can raise, and ultimately limit their effectiveness.

Complicating matters for liberals was the fact that the Supreme Court had ruled in favor of these organizations and their activities, in a famous case that came to be known simply as the Citizens United ruling. On January 21, 2010, the Supreme Court put forth a ruling in *Citizens United v. Federal Elections Commission* that overturned many previous restrictions on campaign contributions. Not surprisingly, this led to rapid growth among such groups on both sides of the political spectrum, and between 2010 and 2012, the number of applications the IRS received seeking 501(c)(4) certification doubled each year.

Officials at the IRS have tried to use this dramatic increase in applications, and the resulting case load, as an excuse for what happened. They have cited "overworked employees," "budget cuts," and "simple error" as the reasons so many conservative groups were held up and denied status, but an examination of the facts shows otherwise.

The record shows that beginning in March 2010, the IRS began to more closely scrutinize certain organizations applying for tax-exempt status under

Section 501(c)(4). Employees were provided "BOLO" (Be On Lookout For) lists, and specifically were told to look more closely at applications from organizations that:

- Contained words such as "Tea Party," "Patriots," "Israel," or "9/12 Project" in their name.
- Advocated education about the United States Constitution or the Bill of Rights.
- Referenced in their application issues that included government spending, government debt, or taxes.
- Were focused on challenging Obamacare, the Patient Protection and Affordable Care Act.
- Were focused on voter fraud or questioned the integrity of federal elections.
- Advocated to "make America a better place to live."
- Contained statements in their case files that criticized how the country is being run.

I don't know about you, but it seems to me that the above list could fairly be characterized as a list of groups who would likely be opposed to Barack Obama as president. Maybe that was just another coincidence.

According to the report by the Inspector General, employees of the "Determinations Unit" of the Cincinnati office of the IRS in May of 2010 began developing this "Be on the Look Out" or BOLO list. Applicants on this list were subjected to intensive scrutiny for the simple reason that their name showed that they were related to the Tea Party movement and other conservative causes. While much of the focus has been on the Cincinnati office, this scrutiny was not limited to that office or those IRS employees. Targeting of conservative groups also took place in two California offices and in the Washington, DC office.

This campaign by the IRS was diabolically successful. Over a two-year period, from April 2010 through April 2012, the IRS put on hold the applications of hundreds of organizations with "Tea Party," "Patriots," or "9/12" in their names, with only four being approved in that entire two-year time frame. Meanwhile dozens of liberal organizations saw their applications sail through without issue.

The National Review was able to obtain instructions given to IRS screeners. These instructions plainly stated that applications of Tea Party groups should be sent "to group 7822" for additional scrutiny. I offer as further proof the following interviews with two of those Cincinnati employees, provided by Darrell Issa, Chairman of the House Oversight and Government Reform Committee, and which can be viewed at breitbart.com, and:

Q: In early 2010, was there a time when you became aware of applications that referenced Tea Party or other conservative groups?

A: In March of 2010, I was made aware.

Q: Okay. Now, was there a point around this time period when [your supervisor] asked you to do a search for similar applications?

A: Yes.

Q: To the best of your recollection, when was this request made?

A: Sometime in early March of 2010.

Q: Did [your supervisor] give you any indication of the need for the search, any more context?

A: He told me that Washington, D.C., wanted some cases.

Q: So as of April 2010, these 40 cases were held at that moment in your group; is that right?

A: Some were.

Q: How many were held there?

A: Less than 40. Some went to Washington, D.C.

Q: Okay. How many went to Washington, D.C.?

A: I sent seven.

Q: So you prepared seven hard copy versions of the applications to go to Washington, D.C.?

A: Correct.

Q: Did he give you any sort of indication as to why he requested you to do that?

A: He said Washington, D.C. wanted seven. Because at one point I believe I heard they were thinking 10, but it came down to seven. I said okay, seven.

Q: How did you decide which seven were sent?

A: Just the first seven.

Q: The first seven to come into the system?

A: Yes.

Q: Did anyone else ever make a request that you send any cases to Washington?

A: [Different IRS employee] wanted to have two cases that she couldn't—
Washington, DC wanted them, but she couldn't find the paper. So she requested me, through an email, to find these cases for her and to send
them to Washington, DC.

Q: When was this, what time frame?

A: I don't recall the time frame, maybe May of 2010.

Q: But just to be clear, she told you the specific names of these applicants.

A: Yes.

Q: And she told you that Washington, DC had requested these two specific
applications be sent to DC.

A: Yes, or parts of them.

Q: Okay. So she asked you to send particular parts of these applications.

A: Mm-hmm.

Q: And that was unusual. Did you say that?

A: Yes.

Q: And she indicated that Washington had requested these specific parts of
these specific applications; is that right?

A: Correct.

Q: So what do you think about this, that allegation has been made, I think as
you have seen in lots of press reports, that there were two rogue agents
in Cincinnati that are sort of responsible for all of the issues that we have
been talking about today. What do you think about those allegations?

A: It's impossible. As an agent we are controlled by many, many people. We
have to submit many, many reports. So the chance of two agents being
rogue and doing things like that could never happen.

Q: And you've heard, I'm sure, news reports about individuals here in Washington saying this is a problem that was originated in and contained in
the Cincinnati office, and that it was the Cincinnati office that was at
fault. What is your reaction to those types of stories?

A: Well, it's hard to answer the question because in my mind I still hear *people saying we were low-level employees, so we were lower than dirt, according to people in D.C. So, take it for what it is. They were basically throwing us underneath the bus.*

Q: *So is it your perspective that ultimately the responsible parties for the decisions that were reported by the IG are not in the Cincinnati office?*

A: *I don't know how to answer that question. I mean, from an agent standpoint, we didn't do anything wrong. We followed directions based on other people telling us what to do.*

Q: *And you ultimately followed directions from Washington; is that correct?*

A: *If direction had come down from Washington, yes.*

Q: *But with respect to the particular scrutiny that was given to Tea Party applications, those directions emanated from Washington; is that right?*

A: *I believe so.*

From an interview with a more senior IRS Cincinnati employee:

Q: *But you specifically recall that the BOLO terms included "Tea Party?"*

A: *Yes, I do.*

Q: *And it was your understanding—was it your understanding that the purpose of the BOLO was to identify Tea Party groups?*

A: *That is correct.*

Q: *Was it your understanding that the purpose of the BOLO was to identify conservative groups?*

A: *Yes, it was.*

Q: *Was it your understanding that the purpose of the BOLO was to identify Republican groups?*

A: *Yes, it was.*

Q: *Earlier I believe you informed us that the primary reason for applying for another job in July [2010] was because of the micromanagement from [Washington, DC, IRS Attorney], is that correct?*

A: *Right. It was the whole Tea Party. It was the whole picture. I mean, it was the micromanagement. The fact that the subject area was extremely sensitive and it was something that I didn't want to be associated with.*

Q: Why didn't you want to be associated with it?

A: For what happened now. I mean, rogue agent? Even though I was taking all my direction from EO Technical [Washington, D.C], I didn't want my name in the paper for being this rogue agent for a project I had no control over.

Q: Did you think there was something inappropriate about what was happening in 2010?

A: Yes. The inappropriateness was not processing these applications fairly and timely.

Q: You have stated you had concerns with the fairness and the timeliness of the application process. Did you have concerns with just the fact that these cases were grouped together and you were the only one handling them?

A: I was the only one handling the Tea Parties, that is correct.

Q: Did that specifically cause you concern?

A: Yes, it did. And I was the only person handling them.

Q: Were you concerned that you didn't have the capacity to process all of the applications in a timely manner?

A: That is correct. And it is just—I mean, like you brought up, the micromanagement, the fact that the topic was just weirdly handled was a huge concern to me.

Not only did conservative groups see their applications held up, they were also harassed and subjected to ridiculously intrusive and likely unconstitutional questioning. Many of these questions they were asked, and the requests they were asked to fulfill, were literally impossible to comply with. Some examples of these questions were:

- To explain in detail the activities at prayer meetings, the content of their prayers, and to provide the percentage of time the group spent on prayer groups as compared with other activities of the organization.

- Some organizations were required to provide examples of "any contracts" or "training material" the groups may have utilized.

- To explain how their activities, including prayer meetings would be considered educational.

- To provide copies of web pages, Blog posts, newsletters, bulletins, flyers, or any other media or literature you have disseminated.
- To provide any groups that may have provided educational services to them, and to provide the names and addresses or any individuals that they have provided educational services to.
- The amounts of any donations, contributions, or grants, the dates they received them, and specifically how they used these donations.
- To provide information not only on their income received from inception to present, but also information on the income they expected to receive in 2012, 2013, and 2014.

As a last insult to Democracy, the IRS also leaked documents pertaining to conservative organizations to openly liberal organizations. During the same time period that tea conservative applications were being scrutinized, the Cincinnati office of the IRS violated policy by releasing nine pending applications from conservative groups to a liberal organization called ProPublica. In addition, the conservative group The National Organization for Marriage claims that the IRS intentionally leaked its 2008 tax return, along with its donor lists, both of which are prohibited by federal law.

Though this scandal didn't become public until the spring of 2013, high ranking IRS officials knew at least as early as mid-2011 that conservative groups were being targeted. In other words, they knew this was happening prior to the 2012 election and chose to do nothing until *after* the election.

When the Inspector General's report finally did come out, it outlined how the IRS had targeted Tea Party and other conservative organizations applying for tax-exempt status. The IG report concluded that:

1. The IRS allowed inappropriate criteria to be developed and stay in place for more than 18 months.
2. This resulted in substantial delays in processing certain applications, in fact work on many of these applications was held up for more than three years.
3. The IRS allowed unnecessary information requests to be issued, and IG report characterized some of these requests as "unnecessary, burdensome questions."

In terms of sheer numbers, there were 292 total applications from conservative groups that were targeted for additional scrutiny, and were held up for 206 to 1,138 days, which in many cases conveniently spanned three years and two election cycles. Of these applications, none were approved, and none were denied. The fact that they were not denied is also important, because a denied application report can be appealed. The IRS chose simply to leave them in limbo until *after* the election.

When you peel away all the rhetoric, the real questions behind all of this are:

- Who in the IRS is responsible for ordering this to take place?
- Was that person given their orders by the Obama White House?

Congress started calling IRS officials to testify in May of 2013 as to how this all started. Former IRS Commissioner Doug Shulman testified that yes, he had frequently visited the White House during the years in question. Actually, it was reported that he was *at the White House 157 times during that period.* However, Mr. Schulman said that in none of those 157 meetings had he ever discussed the targeting of conservatives or any of this with anyone in the White House. Of course not.

Lois Lerner, who headed up the IRS unit that oversaw tax-exempt groups, admitted in remarks she made to the American Bar Association that organizations with "tea party" or "patriot" in their applications for tax-exempt status were singled out for additional reviews. Lerner went on to say that this was all initiated by "low-level workers" in Cincinnati. She dismissed it as "an error in judgment" and declined to answer questions as to how many employees were involved and what if any disciplinary action had been taken. She also, of course, had never discussed the issue with any White House officials.

When called to testify before the House, Lerner opened by stating that she had broken no law and had done nothing wrong, then stated that she was invoking her Fifth Amendment rights not to testify. A substantial debate followed as to whether her opening comments amounted to a waiving of those rights, and Ms. Lerner subsequently offered to testify again in exchange for immunity. My questions are:

- Immunity from what? If you did nothing wrong, why is it necessary to ask for immunity?

- Fifth Amendment is meant to stop self-incrimination. Again, if you did nothing wrong, why do you need it?
- If you don't need to protect yourself, exactly who are you trying to protect?

Liberals have gone to their playbook and pulled out their typical smoke screen on this - mislead and misinform the public, and to do anything that they can to change the narrative. They've tried to assert that liberal groups received the same scrutiny as Tea Party organizations. Many Congressional Democrats sent letters to the Inspector General and appeared anywhere they could on television claiming that liberal groups were equally targeted, and that groups with the words "progressive" or "occupy" in their names received the same kind of treatment.

This is absolutely false.

While it is true that the word "progressive" had appeared in IRS screening documents, and was seen on the "Be on the Look Out" (BOLO) spreadsheet, these terms did not include instructions to IRS employees on how to refer these cases for additional review. While there is extensive evidence to prove that there was a specific process to target conservative groups for additional scrutiny, there is <u>no sign anywhere</u> that the words "Progressive" or "Occupy" would be cause for additional investigation. And the bottom line, according to the IG, is this:

> **<u>Only 30%</u>** of groups whose names contained "progress" or "progressive" were targeted for additional scrutiny.
> **<u>100% of groups</u>** whose names contained "Tea Party," "Patriot," or "9/12" were targeted.

Also, as compared to 292 conservative groups having their applications held up, only 19 liberal groups were delayed. Of those, 6 were denied and 13 were approved. As much as Congressman Elijah Cummings and other democrats want to claim that there was equal scrutiny here, I really can't see how 292–0 equals parity.

As of this writing, 25 Tea Party groups were suing the IRS, Attorney General Eric Holder and senior IRS officials, claiming the Obama administration unlawfully targeted their groups because of their political beliefs. The use of the IRS as a political weapon should frighten and disgust every American, and we can only hope that those responsible are brought to justice.

We have also recently been treated to another round of pathetic videos showing government employees wasting millions of tax dollars. Much as we saw last year with the outlandish GSA conferences where millions in tax dollars were wasted, the IRS spent $50 million on at least 220 conferences between 2010 and 2012.

Given that the IRS is being used as a political tool, will soon become even more powerful as the enforcers of ObamaCare, and has shown that it can't be trusted to either collect or spend our money properly, there is only one logical question:

Isn't it time to do away with the IRS?

As of this writing, there was no smoking gun to prove that Obama or anyone in his White House ordered or knew about what the IRS was doing. Congressman Darrell Issa and his committee were hard at work trying to prove just that, and we can only hope that they somehow find the proof they seek.

We do however have proof that despite his flowery rhetoric, Barack Obama will stoop to just about any depths to win an election.

In his very first race for office, young community organizer Obama was running for a state Senate seat on the south side of Chicago in 1996. He'd helped register thousands of voters (I'm sure all of them legitimate) but it still appeared that he would not only lose, but lose badly.

The incumbent was Alice Palmer, an Africa American woman and a long-time Chicago activist. When it looked clear that she would win the primary against young Barack, he decided to make sure she wouldn't be able to. Obama sent a group to the County Clerk's office to challenge the voting petition signatures of Ms. Palmer and two other challengers.

I don't know how much you know about challenging signatures, but if I challenge a signature and say that this *t* is not crossed or this *i* is not dotted and therefore the name is misspelled, or if I say this signature is not legible, or if I mount any semi-reasonable challenge at all the signature will likely be thrown out. Obama's team was able to get enough signatures *from all three of the other primary candidates* thrown out to invalidate their petition to run, and to get them thrown off the ballot.

In short, since he was going to lose the election, he made sure there would be no election. He ended up running unopposed in the Democratic primary in what was a heavily Democrat district, by making sure that the voters had just one choice. Take some time to do a search on this primary election in 1996, and to read the comments and reactions of some of his opponents. It is a telling glimpse into the character of Barack Obama.

It should surprise no one that in Obama's subsequent elections, there was never what you would exactly call a clean race.

During his primary campaign for the US Senate in 2004 the campaign of his most-feared opponent imploded just a few weeks before polling day. Unsealed divorce papers mysteriously became public, revealing that Blair Hull's former wife had detailed several allegations of verbal and physical abuse, and that she had asked for a restraining order because Hull had allegedly threatened to kill her. In a field of eight, Obama won 53% of the vote.

In the general election that year, Republican candidate Jack Ryan seemed like a viable challenger for the senate seat until his divorce papers were also suddenly unsealed. In those documents it was alleged that Ryan had pressured his ex-wife, Jeri, to go to clubs where people had sex in public. Even though he denied the allegations, Ryan nevertheless dropped out in June, allowing Barack Obama to run unopposed once again, this time for the US Senate.

Anyone else see a pattern here?

To summarize, after seeing that the Tea Party was an effective force in the 2010 mid-terms, someone in the Obama administration decided to limit the Tea Party's effectiveness in 2012 by using the IRS to cut off their funding by denying them tax exempt status. Given the above Obama track record and other conduct we've seen from him, it's reasonable to suspect that he was somehow involved. Whoever gave the order, it's clear that the Obama administration used the vast power of the federal government, specifically the IRS and the powers within the Patriot Act, to help them win in 2012. Maybe.

Those Who Count the Votes Decide Everything

As I mentioned earlier, the famed communist philosopher Joseph Stalin uttered these words decades ago. It stands to reason that if one candidate can control the counting of the votes, there's a pretty good chance that said candidate will triumph.

As I also discussed earlier, it's documented that the SEIU has an exclusive contract with Clark County, Nevada, to "service" their voting machines. It's also documented that in the 2010 midterm elections Harry Reid staged a miraculous comeback, somehow rallying from a 4-point deficit one week before Election Day to a 6-point victory.

It was reported widely that on the night of the 2012 election, 4,000 votes were flipped from incumbent Congressman Allen West to his Democrat challenger. The flipping of those votes changed the results of the election, as Allen West lost his district by less than 2,500 votes. Election officials admitted that the 4,000 votes had initially been read incorrectly, but there was never a full investigation or any actual resolution.

In Marion County, Ohio, a woman named Joan Stevens touched "Mitt Romney" on her touch screen voting machine, but says that the name "Barack Obama" was illuminated. She tried again but again Obama's name lit up. She left the voting booth and reported the problem to an election official, who first said that perhaps Ms. Stevens was not touching the screen properly, and later said that the machine had been checked and was working properly.

There were reports in the New Jersey Democratic primary of votes being miscast for Obama. The Pueblo Colorado Republican Party asked the Secretary of State to investigate dozens of reports of votes cast for Romney that the machine changed to Obama. In Philadelphia, where the history of voting irregularities is second only to Chicago, there were multiple reports in 2008 of machines already having votes on them when the polls first opened.

Among many researchers and experts in the field, there is tremendous concern about the numerous security flaws in electronic voting machines. Reports like the ones above have become more and more common, and there are dozens more incidents that point to the hacking of voting

machines to swap votes between candidates, to reject ballots, and in some cases to accept many more votes from precincts than there are actual *voters*.

J. Alex Halderman, a computer science professor at the University of Michigan who researches voting machine security, said the following:

> *"Every time they are studied, we find further problems. It's simply a matter of reprogramming these machines to be dishonest. That's what we found six years ago and it's still true today, and many of these machines are still in use. A hacker with access to an AccuVote voting machine <u>for just one minute</u> could install the necessary codes to switch votes."*

Researchers at Princeton University, studying the problem in 2008, found that it *took just seven minutes, using simple tools*, to install a different computer program in a voting machine the "would steal votes from one party's candidate and give them to another." The researchers went on to conclude that they had seen "high school science fair projects" that were more sophisticated than what was required to hack some voting machines.

Clearly, the evidence suggests that these voting machines can be reprogrammed to switch votes, and therefore the issue becomes frighteningly simple — *who has access to them?*

In situations where a blatantly liberal organization like the SEIU or some other union's personnel have free and unlimited access, and/or where Democrats have total control of a county or municipality, what's to stop them from programming these machines to their liking?

Given all the reports of votes being switched, apparently nothing.

What's even more disconcerting is the fact that e-voting machines do not produce a paper record for voters in many states because it isn't required by the state. Without paper ballots, there is no paper trail, so no one can go back and conduct an audit to see whether votes were fairly and properly counted.

To help combat this, in 2006 Maryland lawmakers voted to stop using AccuVote machines because of concerns with security and because they did not product a paper record of the votes that were cast. But Governor Martin O'Malley, Democrat, decided NOT to fund the purchase of new voting machines which would indeed provide paper ballots, ensuring that on Election Day 2012 Maryland voters would vote on the old machines, which would not produce a paper trail. Guess what? Obama won Maryland.

There were reports by Wikileaks in 2008 that the Obama campaign engaged in what they termed massive ballot box stuffing in Ohio and Philadelphia, either through tampering with voting machines or through simple fraud. Obama got 85% of the vote in Philadelphia in 2008. In 2012, despite record homicides, record unemployment, and a city going bankrupt, Obama received 99% of the vote throughout much of Philadelphia, and in some Divisions 100%. Was this the result of even more voters deciding that they wanted Obama in office, or did they simply improve on their ballot stuffing efforts in 2008?

Speaking of 2008, remember all those reports that Romney received fewer votes than McCain had in 2008?

Not true.

In truth, it was *Obama* who received about 2 million fewer votes than in 2008, the first president *ever reelected* with a smaller number of votes. Mitt Romney actually got about *2.2 million more votes* than John McCain received in 2008, an increase of nearly 4%.

In Ohio specifically, McCain received 2,501,855 votes in 2008, and in 2012 Mitt Romney received 2,593,777. This represented an increase for Romney of 91,922 votes, a 3.7% increase, virtually the same increase as the national increase.

HOWEVER, in the seven Ohio counties we previously discussed that went for Obama—Cuyahoga, Franklin, Hamilton, Lorain, Summit, Mahoning, and Lucas—Mitt Romney did receive fewer votes than did John McCain in 2008. Far fewer. In fact:

- Romney got 47,657 fewer votes than McCain did in 2008 in these seven counties.
- This represents a 5.3% reduction for the Republican candidate, *while the rest of the state and the rest of the country showed about a 4% increase.*
- If you subtract these seven counties, the rest of the state of Ohio SHOWED AN INCREASE OF 139,579 VOTES, AN 8.7% IN-CREASE for Mitt Romney versus McCain in 2008.

We keep hearing that Romney lost the election because he didn't get out his base. These figures demonstrate that this is clearly nonsense.

The question we need to ask is: How could 81 counties in a state show an 8.7% increase in votes for the Republican candidate in 2012 versus 2008, while 7 counties had a 5.3% drop—a 14% difference.

Was the Republican base less energized in 2012 than it was in 2008?

Absolutely not, in fact all polls showed Republicans far more energized in 2012 than in 2008, and that support for Obama had dropped substantially among virtually all demographics. Both of these predictions turned out to be true nationally, as Obama received far fewer votes versus 2008 and Romney received far more than McCain.

So how could these seven Democratic controlled counties buck this trend? A very plausible answer is:

> In these seven Democrat-controlled counties, votes for Romney were somehow switched, thrown out, or in some way not counted.

Is it possible that thousands of Romney votes were switched in these counties? That certainly makes more sense that the explanation that an energized Republican base for some mysterious reason decided not to turn out in counties that just happen to be controlled by Democrats.

What Democrats have been billing as an "inability to turn out his base" as the reason for the Romney loss may have indeed been a case of his base's votes being switched.

We saw these ridiculous margins for Obama, the 99% to 100% share of the vote that we recounted earlier in this book, strictly in counties and cities that were controlled by Democrats. Based on some of the reports alleging that voting machines changed votes from Mitt Romney to Barack Obama, it is entirely possible that this is how they achieved those results. It is entirely possible that the Obama campaign, knowing they were in trouble, decided to employ a strategy of changing votes in those precincts where they had control to bring in enough votes to overcome their vast losses elsewhere in these states.

The facts are that we know machines can be reprogrammed to change votes, we have multiple reports of it's happening, and we know that SEIU and other union personnel have free access to these machines in many places where Democrats also have control of the process. That's very possibly how Obama was able to achieve results in many precincts of 500+ to 0, or 3400 to 300, a reasonable explanation as to why Republican turnout was so much lower in many of those areas, and that's very likely a key reason he was able to "defeat" Mitt Romney.

Eric Holder and the DONJ (Department of No Justice)

I confess that I'm not a great student of Attorneys General past, but I have to believe that there's never been a more disgraceful example of a chief law enforcement officer than Eric Holder. Based on his repeated and disgraceful abuses of power and his total lack of respect for the law and our constitution, I will refer to his department as the DONJ.

With specific regard to the reelection of Barack Obama in 2012, Eric Holder fulfilled two very critical roles:

- He utilized his power to do everything he could to block voter ID laws, any effort to clean up voter rolls, or any other attempts to curtail voter fraud; and also provided cover for anyone who wanted to take part in any voting irregularities on behalf of Barack Obama.
- He used the power of the Patriot Act to target journalists who dared to criticize Obama or his policies, and to gather information on citizens for their "databases."

Eric Holder has been an absolute zealot in his fight against the requirement of a photo ID in order to vote. He has compared these laws to the old "poll tax" laws that were designed to discourage voting by black Americans years ago. Holder is one of the many Democrats who openly declare that anyone who favors voter ID laws is simply a racist.

There was a portion of the Voting Rights Act of 1965, which Holder had made great use of, that essentially said that ANY state with a history of previous racial discrimination had to "pre-clear" any new election laws with the federal government. This clearly unconstitutional portion of the law was finally overturned by the Supreme Court in June of 2013.

Holder called this a "deeply disappointing and flawed" decision, and vowed to "use every tool" at his disposal to fight against it. He then had the DONJ file suit against the state of Texas and their proposed redistricting because HE felt it was racially discriminatory.

Never mind that the Constitution clearly states that the individual states have power over their elections, and that the Supreme Court decision in *Shelby v. Holder* was absolutely, constitutionally the correct decision by the law. It didn't fit Eric Holder's view of the world.

In July 2013, Holder went even further in his actions against the state of Texas, challenging their proposed voter ID law. In a speech to the NAACP, he said:

> *"Let me be clear: We will not allow political pretexts to disenfranchise American citizens of their most precious rights. I can assure you that the Justice Department's efforts to uphold and enforce voting rights will remain aggressive."*

He again referred to the requirement of a photo ID as akin to a "poll tax," trying to incite his audience by taking them back to a time in America 50 years ago when such laws existed. For the record, the Supreme Court in 1966 declared such laws unconstitutional, and the 24th Amendment abolished any such taxes in 1964.

I have to assume that playing the race card in this manner was one of the "tools" Holder was referring to above. Any time Eric Holder and other Liberals feel that a law requiring an ID may actually be passed, they will always label as racism any such attempt to require a photo ID to vote.

This is all a diversion. Laws requiring people to present government-issued photo IDs when voting are generally favored by Republicans and opposed by Holder and many Democrats for one simple reason:

Because they make voter fraud more difficult.

The number of states that have tried to implement such laws only to have Eric Holder and the DONJ stand in their way goes on and on. The state of

South Carolina had to file a federal lawsuit to overturn a DONJ decision blocking the state's new photo ID requirement. Texas is currently embroiled in their fight, and Holder and the DONJ were active in challenging voter ID laws in Wisconsin, and Pennsylvania. Ohio's Secretary of State sent a letter to Holder asking for help to clean up their voter rolls – shockingly there was no response.

The DONJ, with help from Democratic Governors and sympathetic judges, worked to block voter ID laws passed by the duly elected legislatures in at least 14 states in the period leading up to the 2012 election. In Arizona, Florida, Maine, Michigan, Minnesota, Missouri, Montana, New Hampshire, North Carolina, Ohio, Pennsylvania, South Carolina, Texas, and Wisconsin, Holder and friends worked diligently to ensure that this simple tool to help bring about legitimate elections would not be in place.

You can conduct your own internet search on the number of times that Holder has intervened against state laws that are intended to ensure integrity in our election process. This extensive body of evidence, in addition to the testimony and statements of people in his own department, make it clear that Holder's intention is to use the Department of Justice more for political gain than for the pursuit of Justice.

In addition to its efforts to fight against the requirement of a voter ID, the Holder DONJ has been equally active in its mission to stop states from cleaning up their voter rolls. Think back to the efforts by the Holder DONJ to stop the state of Florida from purging its voter rolls of ineligible voters. The state of Florida took a small sample and found 100 illegally registered voters, *of whom 46 voted in the last election.*

> For those Democrats who say that these fraudulently registered voters *"hardly ever vote,"* I'm not a statistician, but I'm fairly certain that 46% is statistically more than *"hardly ever."*

To help them clean up their voter rolls, Florida asked the Department of Homeland Security for the official roles of US Citizens, lists to which they are legally entitled. The Obama administration refused to provide them, forcing the state of Florida to sue in order to get them.

The Motor Voter law was passed in 1993, and the DONJ has certainly supported some portions of the law, pushing to maximize turnout of Democrats in 2012 by filing "motor voter" suits across the country, complaining that state agencies weren't circulating voter registration forms in social service agencies.

However, <u>no effort</u> was made by the DONJ to enforce the section of the law (Section 8) that requires states to clean voter rolls to get rid of dead persons, felons, and other ineligible voters. In point of fact, they have done just the opposite.

Section 8 has almost never been enforced despite the immense potential for fraud caused by inaccurate and unreliable voter registration lists. The evidence would suggest that Holder and other Democrats fight its enforcement *because of* that very thing—the immense potential for voter fraud provided by all of these fraudulent registrations. Put bluntly, the Obama/Holder DONJ has refused to enforce Section 8, and has engaged in what is known as selective enforcement, only acting on the parts of the law that it favors.

Not surprisingly, there was never a single Section 8 case filed under Bill Clinton either, and when the Bush administration filed the first case in 2005 it was raked over the coals for doing so. And, as stated earlier, the next case filed by the Obama/Holder DONJ administration will be the first case filed.

The DONJ to date *has not filed a single case* to enforce Section 8, even though literally hundreds of counties in many states have the same discrepancies between voter rolls and eligible voters as those cited earlier. Even through benign neglect or through planned inactivity, there is no effort by the DONJ to see to it that these problems are corrected.

Based on the evidence, it is not benign neglect. According to a report on the Civil Rights Division of the DONJ by the inspector general, *ten witnesses* told the IG that one of Obama's political appointees, Julie Fernandes, had specifically told Division staff that the administration *was not interested in pursuing any cases under Section 8 because it did not expand voter access.*

In 2010, Christopher Coates, the former chief of the Voting Section at the Division, recommended that at least eight different states be investigated for violations of Section 8. To no one's surprise, his recommendations were ignored by the Obama/Holder DONJ. Eventually, Coates was forced out of his position as a career manager at the Division because of his stubborn and *ridiculous* insistence that they were supposed to enforce the law. I guess he never got the memo.

When discussing the rampant voter fraud that's taking place, I'm often asked why people wouldn't be afraid of going to jail if they were caught. First of all, as we've shown throughout this book, these activities often take place in strongly controlled democratic precincts. That protection, plus having Eric Holder in charge of the DONJ, provides all the cover that people will ever need.

Since he took office, Eric Holder has demonstrated time and again that he will not pursue cases of voting irregularities against those who support Barack Obama. Gentlemen, start your voter fraud.

Following the 2008 election, Eric Holder refused to proceed with the prosecution of the two black panthers who stood outside a Philadelphia polling place, allegedly to intimidate white voters, or as some said to stop anyone from interfering with the fraud taking place within. Holder said that to proceed with the case would "demean my people."

Holder is obliged to enforce federal election laws in an objective, non-partisan, race-neutral manner, yet in 2010 a whistleblower came forward and said that under Holder the department had a policy of not pursuing election fraud cases involving people of color.

A man by the Christian Adams, who was Coates's co-counsel, eventually came forward and testified to Congress as a whistleblower. Adams apparently clashed with his superiors at Justice over his views supporting "race-neutral enforcement" of the Voting Rights Act. Adams testified that Eric Holder's DONJ had made it clear to people in the Division that no charges regarding voting improprieties would be brought against people of color.

To further support Adam's testimony, Tom Perez, who headed up the Civil Rights division, told the IG that in his opinion, Section 5 of the Voting Rights Act *does not protect white voters from racial discrimination.*

I've spoken a good deal about Eric Holder's world view, and one of the things that undoubtedly helped shape that goes back 50 years.

On June 11, 1963, a young woman by the name of Vivian Malone, along with a young man named James Hood, enrolled for summer classes at the University of Alabama. Governor George Wallace famously stood in the doorway to stop them until he was removed by the National Guard.

Vivian Malone Jones's brother-in-law is now our Attorney General. Eric Holder is married to Vivian's sister, Dr. Sharon Malone. There can be no doubt that this historic event is one of many that helped shape his views and opinions, and also may help explain why he does some of the things he does.

I say this with no disrespect to the late Mrs. Malone Jones. I respect the fact that she went on to become the first African American woman to graduate from the University of Alabama, and I admire her courage not just for her actions that day in June of 1963, but for enduring what I'm sure wasn't always a pleasant college experience.

My point is that this and other events do help explain how Eric Hold came to view America the way he apparently does and to have the beliefs he apparently has. An explanation, however, is not a justification, and what can't be justified is that this Attorney General appears to follow those beliefs rather than enforcing the rule of law.

All of the above actions support my earlier statement - that Eric Holder is not fit to serve as the nation's chief law enforcement officer. His mission to fight against voter ID laws, to fight against attempts to clean up voter rolls, to dismiss any wrongdoing by those he politically agrees with, and the testimony and statements from people in his own department, can lead to only one logical conclusion. Eric Holder views our voting rights, and has run that section of our Department of Justice, not based on the law, not based on our constitution and his oath of office to defend it, but rather based on his own (and Barack Obama's) worldview and political beliefs.

The Orwellian Actions of Obama and Holder

Holder and presumably Barack Obama did not limit their attempts to influence the 2012 elections strictly to the voting booth. They apparently made the determination that they could use the power of the federal government and its ability to monitor the activity of the American people to their benefit as well.

When we passed the Patriot Act, even though I believe it was passed at the time to help protect us from terrorist attacks, I voiced concern that if we ever had a President who wanted to use the power of the Patriot Act to target American citizens, perhaps for his own political gain, they could do so. We now appear to have such a president and such an Attorney General.

Section 215 of the Patriot Act, known as the business records provision, is the section used to justify the review of essentially ALL domestic communications under the NSA's massive PRISM program. To gain access to these communications, the government must request them through the FISA court, short for Foreign Intelligence Surveillance Court.

In 2012, the Obama administration made 212 such requests, which represented a 1000 percent increase over requests made four years earlier by the Bush Administration. In 2011, FBI Director Robert Muller told Congress that the FBI began relying much more heavily on Section 215 requests in *2010*.

Wait a minute. Isn't that right around the time the Democrats got hammered in the 2010 midterm elections? And isn't that about the same time that the IRS started targeting Tea Party organizations.

Democrats have been bragging in recent years about these tremendous "databases" they have created to reach out to their voting base. It makes me wonder what else exactly is in these databases, and what kind of information they have been gathering not just on their voters, but more importantly on people who are not their voters.

Obama has defended his NSA spying on American citizens by claiming that the tracking of billions of phone and Internet records from millions of Americans has been "a circumscribed, narrow system," and has said that each and every intercept is potentially related to a terrorist investigation.

I hate to sound cynical, but given this administration's track record of abusing its authority (Fast & Furious, IRS/Tea Party, ignoring laws passed by Congress) and blatantly lying about national security (4 dead Americans in Benghazi murdered because of a video) I'm a bit skeptical.

Is there some reason, some national security reason, that the Obama administration would have increased the number of FISA requests tenfold, from about 20 under Bush in 2008 to over 200 in 2012? I don't recall any extraordinary national security events in 2012, other than Benghazi, and as we all know that was not a terrorist attack. It was a spontaneous protest over a video.

Experts tell us that Obama and the NSA are not really reviewing "content" of our phone calls and emails, but rather are collecting what is known as "Metadata," which is really data about data. This may be true, but they can tell where the calls are going and coming from, and where the emails are going and coming from.

Google and other search engines are capable of sorting through millions of pages in seconds, and we have to assume that the government can as well. In fact, we know that they can, because the original intent of this program was to sort through billions of calls and emails to find those that went back and forth with known terrorists or terror groups. My question is:

> If we can target communications with those legitimate enemies of our country, why would we assume that an administration could not target its political enemies if they were so inclined?

What would stop the government, if they wanted to do so, from reviewing calls or emails that went to or came from certain other mailboxes or phone numbers based on some other filter, other than terror related? What if, for example, they wanted to know who had exchanged emails or phone calls with a Tea Party group, or a Right to Life group, or an NRA group?

You could learn a great deal about people based on these communications. From there, it would just a hop, skip, and a jump to be creating "lists," either "friendly" or "unfriendly," that could be kept for future reference.

It was revealed in August of 2013 that the documents released by Edward Snowden showed that the NSA had broken privacy rules or overstepped its legal authority *thousands of times each year since 2008*. The Washington Post reported that an NSA audit in May 2012 outlined 2,776 incidents in the preceding 12 months of unauthorized collection or distribution of legally protected communications.

The Obama administration has clearly shown that they aren't above using the power of the federal government to attack their political opponents, as we've seen in the recent IRS scandal. They've bragged about the immense databases they are compiling to use in future elections. Given their track record, and their huge escalation in this program, it is not unreasonable to wonder what information they are gathering and exactly what they intend to use it for.

Another shameful example of the abuse of his power, and yet another reason that Eric Holder should resign, was the targeting of Fox News reporter James Rosen. In short, Eric Holder signed a letter authorizing the surveillance of Rosen under totally false pretenses.

The letter that Holder signed authorizing this illegal surveillance stated that Rosen may be guilty of and possibly charged as a criminal co-conspirator in violation of the Espionage Act. They also had to classify him as a "flight risk," in order to obtain a warrant allowing them to read his emails and access his phone records. Holder also insisted that the warrant remain classified, asking the court to order Google not to notify Rosen that they had handed over his e-mails.

There is nothing to indicate that the DONJ had any evidence whatsoever that Rosen was breaking the law. What appears to be true is that Holder decided to illegally spy on a United States citizen solely because he worked for a network unfriendly to Obama, and had conducted investigations and done reporting that were politically at odds with the Obama administration.

Holder at one point testified to the House Judiciary Committee that he himself had not been involved in any potential prosecution of journalists. It was just a few days later that news broke that he had personally signed off on the Rosen surveillance – you can see his signature right there. One of two things is true:

- Holder lied to Congress during his testimony.
- He did not bother to read the letter signed.
- For those of you keeping score at home, both of those things are bad.

Though Fox News is certainly Administration Enemy #1 for Obama and Holder, apparently no reporter is safe if they have the temerity to report on stories that put the White House or DONJ in a bad light. According to reports, a CBS News reporter's computer was remotely accessed by an "unauthorized party" several times late last year. This was first reported by CBS News, citing an analysis by an outside cyber security firm.

According to a report by CBS News spokeswoman Sonya McNair:

- Washington reporter Sharyl Attkisson's computer "was accessed by an unauthorized, external, unknown party on multiple occasions late in 2012."
- Forensic analysis showed the hacker appeared to have searched and extracted data, and then "used sophisticated methods" to cover up the unauthorized activity.
- CBS News is "taking steps to identify the responsible party and their method of access."

Attkisson had reportedly extensively on Operation Fast and Furious, as well as on the attack in September on the US outpost in Benghazi, in which the US ambassador to Libya and three other Americans were killed. Perhaps not coincidentally, both of these stories are a source of great embarrassment, if not outright lawlessness, by the Obama administration and the DONJ.

Attkisson, in an interview with Bill O'Reilly, stated that the hacking began in February 2011 when she was reporting on stories critical of the Obama administration, including the gun operation Fast & Furious. She stated that both her work and her home computers may have been targeted, and that she and CBS were working hard to identify those guilty of doing so.

Though these are the most recent, they are by no means the only examples of the Holder DONJ using its power to unlawfully attack a political enemy. In May 2013, the DOJ Inspector General published a report confirming that a former US Attorney for Arizona, Dennis Burke, had leaked a document intended to smear Operation Fast and Furious scandal whistleblower John Dodson. The IG's report concluded that "Burke's conduct in disclosing the Dodson memorandum was inappropriate for a Department employee and wholly unbefitting a US Attorney."

Not at the DONJ.

One of those found to be smearing Mr. Dodson was Tracy Schmaler, the Director of the Department's Office of Public Affairs. She was forced to resign her position at the DONJ after it was discovered that:

- She worked with leftwing advocacy group Media Matters for America.

- She was charged with smearing whistleblowers, members of Congress, and the media.

- Her targets: anyone who dared to investigate any of the Holder DONJ scandals.

If you felt at the beginning of this chapter that referring to Holder's DOJ as the DONJ was in any way unfair, hopefully you are now persuaded otherwise. If not, following are a few more of what I'll just call "Eric Holder's Greatest Hits":

- When still working in the Clinton Administration, then-Assistant Attorney General Holder created a controversy surrounding the pardon of Democratic donor Marc Rich, at the time on the FBI's "most wanted" list. *Even the New York Times* called it a "shocking abuse" of power.

- The holder Justice Department decided to intervene on behalf of a Muslim school teacher in Cook County, Illinois, who said the school district was guilty of religious bias when it denied her request for a 19-day paid leave of absence to go to Mecca. Incredibly, with the DONJ's help, the district was forced to settle the suit and pay the teacher $75,000 for a purported violation of the Civil Rights Act of

1964. The teacher had worked at the school for only a year, and the leave she wanted was not even in the limits for teachers under the union contract.

- The Justice Department has waged war against state immigration laws, filing suit against Utah over a law that permits police to detain individuals they suspect are illegal aliens. Utah was the fourth state to be sued over immigration laws since Obama/Holder came to power, with the first suit and most famous filed against Arizona. When appearing before a congressional committee concerning the Arizona law, Holder astonishingly admitted he hadn't even read the law he was seeking to overturn.
- Holder appointed known Obama supporters to investigate the White House Security leaks.
- Last but not least, there is the egregious case known as "Fast & Furious." The House Oversight and Government Reform Committee had to repeatedly subpoena the Obama Administration over the program that sent thousands of guns to Mexico under a Department of Justice botched program. Committee Chairman
- Darrell Issa (R-CA) charged that Eric Holder provided "misleading information" to Congress in May when he suspiciously said he first learned of the program.

The above list represents only a small fraction of cases where Eric Holder seems to have acted based on his view of the world, and on his view of Justice, not based on the law. Holder seems to believe that his job is to establish justice (or at least his view of it) rather than enforce the laws. At least 59 members of Congress have called for Holder's resignation.

In Eric Holder, we have an AG who feels that his job is to fight against voter ID laws, fight against any effort to clean up voter rolls, be sure everyone (who supports Obama) knows they can engage in voting irregularities without prosecution, and utilize his department to target members of the media who dare to criticize his department or the President, or anyone who opposes their policies. It's all just part of how Obama won reelection in 2012. Maybe.

My thesis for this book is that maybe, just maybe, not every vote cast for Barack Obama in this election was a legitimate vote, and that the Obama administration engaged in a variety of at least questionable if not illegal tactics to steal the reelection. As a brief review of what we've seen:

- Romney won 71 of 88 counties in Ohio yet lost the state.
- Romney won 54 of 67 counties in Florida yet lost the state.
- Romney won 54 of 67 counties in Pennsylvania yet lost the state.
- Romney won 87 of 134 municipalities in Virginia yet lost the state.
- Romney won 15 of 17 municipalities in Nevada yet lost the state.
- Romney won 23 of 33 counties in Oregon yet lost the state.
- Dozens of precincts in Philadelphia and Cleveland that showed thousands of votes for Obama and 0 for Romney.
- Hundreds of precincts with more than 99% of the vote for Obama.
- At least 3 states where Republican poll watchers were thrown out, all key battleground states.
- Dramatically higher turnout in Philadelphia divisions where Republican poll workers were illegally removed.
- A Democratic official who said she didn't "care what the law says" about throwing them out in Philadelphia.
- More than 95% of the vote for Obama in Columbus, Ohio, where True the Vote poll watchers were denied access.
- Poll watchers who had registered complaints during early voting denied access on Election Day in Florida.
- Poll watchers who witnessed numerous examples of illegal voting, especially in key states such as Ohio, Florida, and Virginia.
- Election judges allowing illegal voting in many forms in Ohio, Florida, and Virginia.
- Hundreds of thousands of known false voter registrations.
- Hundreds of thousands of voters registered in multiple states.
- Hundreds of thousands of voters with duplicate registrations.
- Hundreds of counties with more people registered than there are voting eligible citizens.
- Incredible margins for Obama in precincts and counties where Democrats have control.
- Incredible margins for Obama in absentee ballots.

- Incredible margins for Obama in early voting.
- States with very prolonged voting periods showing extremely high turn-out, along with much higher margins for Obama.
- Multiple examples of votes being flipped or switched by electronic voting machines, in Florida, Nevada, and Colorado.
- A Congressional race in Florida that may well have been turned by 4000 switched votes.
- Clear evidence that programming voting machines to switch votes is very possible.
- A county in Nevada where the SEIU services voting machines.
- 7 counties in Ohio, controlled by Democrats, that somehow showed about a 5% drop in votes for Romney, while 81 counties showed almost a 9% increase.
- A citizen in Oregon advertising to pay $20 for your unused ballot.
- Obama murals on the walls in Philadelphia polling places.
- Democrats crossing state lines to illegally vote in Ohio.
- Democrats registering in more than 1 county in Arizona.
- Poll workers turning in false absentee ballots.
- Sons voting as fathers, after the father voted early.
- Voters showing up at the polls and voting more than once.
- Multiple votes seen to be cast under one name.
- A man who couldn't vote because someone had already voted under his name.
- People voting who can't even provide their address.
- Democratic poll workers helping them remember it.
- People voting who are clearly not the person on their ID.
- Busloads of voters pouring into precincts controlled by Democrats.
- Unbelievably similar results in Democratic counties in key states.
- Examples of votes being double counted.
- One live nun casting a ballot for one dead nun.
- A voter who voted in his precinct then left and voted in another.
- Hundreds of non-citizens voting illegally.
- Convicted felons voting illegally.
- A Congressman's son in Virginia giving tutorials on how to vote illegally.
- A member of the Massachusetts legislature who distributed and submitted fraudulent absentee ballots in his own election.

- An administration that wants millions more on food stamps to help buy their votes.
- An administration that wants millions more on disability to help buy their votes.
- An administration that passed ObamaCare under a torrent of lies, knowing that it would create millions more Americans that were dependent on the federal government, hence ensuring their votes.
- Nearly $200 million dollars in campaign contributions coming in for Obama just before the election, 98% of which can't be traced.
- The Obama campaign openly soliciting for foreign donations.
- Evidence that many foreigners did contribute to the Obama campaign.
- Evidence that the Obama campaign failed to utilize the most basic of fundraising safeguards, deliberately paying millions of dollars more in fees to receive less information on donors.
- An IRS that selectively targeted organizations that contained the words "Tea Party" in their name.
- An IRS that selectively targeted organizations that contained the words "Patriots" in their name.
- An IRS that selectively targeted organizations that contained the words "9/12" in their name.
- An IRS that selectively targeted organizations that talked about educating people on the Constitution or the Bill of rights.
- An IRS that selectively targeted organizations that talked about educating people on reduced government spending, lower taxes, and less government debt.
- An IRS that selectively targeted organizations that talked about Obamacare being bad for America.
- An IRS that selectively targeted organizations that talked about the importance of stopping voter fraud, and ensuring the integrity of our elections.
- An IRS that selectively targeted organizations or individuals that decided to exercise their First amendment rights and criticize the Obama administration.
- An AG who fights against voter ID laws.
- An AG who fights against clearing voter rolls of dead people and other improperly registered voters.
- An AG who has made it clear that his department will not pursue voting irregularities by "people of color."

- An AG who assigns people in his department to specifically target their enemies.
- An AG who spies, under false pretenses, on reporters who dare to report the unflattering truth about their administration.
- An AG that selectively enforces election laws based not on the law but apparently on his preferences and his beliefs.

Are you beginning to think that maybe, just maybe, Mitt Romney should have been inaugurated on January 21, 2013?

The bigger questions are, what is at stake, and what do we do now?

The answers to those questions are, everything, and everything we can.

Our country was created as a representative Republic, one in which the majority of the people determines the course of events. The words "of the people, by the people, and for the people" tell us that the collective will of the majority of the people is meant to be what drives the policies and direction of our nation.

In the 2012 election, I don't believe that's what happened. I believe the above evidence shows that the Obama administration and the Democratic Party employed the following tactics in 2012:

- Fabricated tens of thousands of votes in key states.
- Raised hundreds of millions in questionable funding.
- Used the IRS to illegally suppress the efforts of their opponents.
- Targeted those who opposed them for illegal surveillance.
- Utilized the Department of Justice to run interference.

By employing these tactics, I believe they were able to literally steal an election, and in doing so to thwart the will of the majority of the people.

I thought about entitling this book *The Stealing of the Vote* because it reminded me of the title from the movie *The Silence of the Lambs*. In that movie, they spoke of how the lambs were silent on their way to the slaughter. In a similar way, if we remain silent and do nothing about these threats to the legitimacy of our elections, we are doomed to see this fraud and this corruption repeated again and again.

If Americans who care about the future of our elections, and the future of this country, do not rise up and stop this, it will most certainly happen again and again. As Edmund Burke one said:

If we don't act, if we don't fight to stop what happened in 2012, evil will triumph again. Some may be thinking it's wrong to use the term "evil" in reference to the recent election, and what this administration and other Democrats are doing, but there is a simple logic that makes it absolutely justifiable.

I genuinely believe that God was present in 1776, and He guided the men who created what became this great nation. I believe it was God's will and his plan for America to become the defender of freedom and liberty, and the defender of what is good in this world. Any attempt, therefore, to radically change America, to radically alter what has been this great force for good, can only be labeled as evil.

If America continues down its current path, someday soon we will lose the power to fulfill this role. We will no longer have either the will or the ability to defend freedom around the world. Mark my words, when that day comes, when America can no longer defend freedom and liberty around the world, we'll lose our ability to defend it here at home as well.

If you believe in all that made this country great, and understand that we are now moving away from that, you must know what the inevitable result will be. We will be Greece, or France, with one important distinction—neither of those countries is counted on in the world to be America.

If you understand this, if you understand the dangers our country now faces, and if you fear for what's going to become of the country our children will grow up in, then you know we've got to do something, and soon.

America didn't happen by accident. There was never a nation like it before, and there have been none like it since. God's hand provided our founders with the principles that created it, and good people have defended those principles for over 200 years.

What has always made America great, what made it unique, is that the power was held by the people. The collective will of the people is what determined America's future. If our elections are fraudulent, the people lose that ability, we lose the ability to hold our leaders accountable with our vote, we lose the power. If we allow that to happen, then America as we know it is no more.

Don't listen to those who say we must accept this. We all need to take a stand to ensure that all elections in America really do reflect the genuine will of the people.

If we fail, the great country we were blessed to inherit will be lost to future generations forever. If we fail, there will never be another government "of the people." There will never be another America.